REFRAMING

Other Fortress Press Books
by Donald Capps

Deadly Sins and Saving Virtues

Life Cycle Theory and Pastoral Care

Pastoral Care and Hermeneutics

REFRAMING

A NEW METHOD IN PASTORAL CARE

Donald Capps

FORTRESS PRESS   **Minneapolis**

REFRAMING
A New Method in Pastoral Care

Scripture quotations unless otherwise noted are from the Revised Standard Version of the Bible, copyright © 1946, 1952, and 1971 by the Division of Christian Education of the National Council of Churches.

Excerpt from "What Will You Do, God, When I Die?" from *Poems From the Book of Hours* by Ranier Maria Rilke, copyright 1941 by New Directions Publishing Corporation. Reprinted by permission of New Directions Publishing Corporation. From *The Book of Hours* by Rainer Maria Rilke, translated by A. L. Peck, edited by Eudo C. Mason. Reprinted by permission of The Hogarth Press.

Cover and interior design: Ned Skubic
Cover photo: Ned Skubic Stock Photos

Library of Congress Cataloging-in-Publication Data

Capps, Donald.　78356297　BV
　　Reframing : a new method in pastoral care / Donald Capps.　4012.2
　　　　p. cm.
　　Includes bibliographical references.　·C275
　　ISBN 0-8006-2413-0
　　1. Pastoral counseling.　I. Title.　1990
　BV4012.2.C275 1990
　253.5—dc20　89-37499
　　　　　　　　　　　　　　　　　　　　　　　　　　CIP

The paper used in this publication meets the minimum requirements of American National Standard for Information Sciences—Permanence of Paper for Printed Library Materials, ANSI Z349.48-1984. ∞™

Manufactured in the U.S.A.　AF 1-2413

94　93　92　91　90　1　2　3　4　5　6　7　8　9　10

to the memory of
Walter Holden Capps Sr.
and
Linn Beidler Capps

CONTENTS

Acknowledgments

William Lord, of Toronto School of Theology, deserves special thanks for pointing out to me that my earlier work on the parables of Jesus and pastoral marriage counseling could be developed further with the reframing theory and techniques developed at the Brief Therapy Center of the Mental Research Institute in Palo Alto, California. Frank Rogers, a doctoral candidate at Princeton Theological Seminary, whetted my appetite for reframing theory through seminar papers. I also want to thank an anonymous Master of Divinity student at Princeton Theological Seminary who graciously agreed to my use of his case report. I am most grateful to John A. Hollar, editorial director of Fortress Press books, for his personal supportiveness and very expert guidance, to Timothy G. Staveteig, my book editor at Fortress Press, for his invaluable refinements of the manuscript, to Reneé Fall, associate editor at Fortress Press, and to Sarah Turner Hamilton for preparing the indexes. I am also grateful to President Thomas W. Gillespie, the administrative staff, my faculty colleagues and students for making Princeton Theological Seminary a nice place to work, and to my wife, Karen, for her loyalty and friendship. This book is dedicated to the memory of my paternal grandfather and his brother: the one taught me the value of wisdom, the other showed me the joys of folly.

Quotations from the Book of Job are from Norman C. Habel's translation in his commentary, *The Book of Job* (Philadelphia: The Westminster Press, 1985). All other biblical citations are from the Revised Standard Version.

Then two harlots came to the king, and stood before him. The one woman said, "Oh, my lord, this woman and I dwell in the same house; and I gave birth to a child while she was in the house. Then on the third day after I was delivered, this woman also gave birth; and we were alone; there was no one else with us in the house, only we two were in the house. And this woman's son died in the night, because she lay on it. And she arose at midnight, and took my son from beside me, while your maidservant slept, and laid it in her bosom, and laid her dead son in my bosom. When I rose in the morning to nurse my child, behold, it was dead; but when I looked at it closely in the morning, behold, it was not the child that I had borne." But the other woman said, "No, the living child is mine, and the dead child is yours." The first said, "No, the dead child is yours, and the living child is mine." Thus they spoke before the king.

Then the king said, "The one says, 'This is my son that is alive, and your son is dead'; and the other says, 'No; but your son is dead, and my son is the living one.'" And the king said, "Bring me a sword." So a sword was brought before the king. And the king said, "Divide the living child in two, and give half to the one, and half to the other." Then the woman whose son was alive said to the king, because her heart yearned for her son, "Oh, my lord, give her the living child, and by no means slay it." But the other said, "It shall be neither mine nor yours; divide it." Then the king answered and said, "Give the living child to the first woman, and by no means slay it; she is its mother."

1 Kings 3:16-27

Introduction

The pastoral care and counseling movement of the 1950s and 1960s has been roundly attacked in recent years. Some critics have claimed that it is virtually bankrupt, that the movement has over-emphasized the secular psychotherapies and psychological sciences, and has neglected the theological sciences. Some have charged that the movement has bought into individualism and the therapeutic culture and has given the faith community very short shrift, that it has subscribed to the values of contemporary society, and has failed to give adequate attention to Christian ethical and moral principles. These critics—proponents of the "new" pastoral theology, including Charles Gerkin, Don Browning, and James Poling—see themselves as providing pastoral care and counseling with a much-needed theological, ecclesial, and ethical foundation.

Some of this criticism of the pastoral counseling movement is unfair and overdrawn, based on a somewhat inaccurate picture of what was actually written and practiced in the 1950s and 1960s. Much of it, however, is warranted and welcome. The enterprise of pastoral theology is currently experiencing a renaissance, and promising new directions are being charted. Yet, in spite of these new developments, nothing new has emerged at the basic level of technique.

One of the most exciting features of the pastoral care and counseling movement of the 1950s and 1960s was that new methods and techniques were being proposed, experimented with, assessed, and evaluated. By the mid-1960s, there were enough techniques available for Howard Clinebell to write a basic textbook in pastoral counseling that set forth a variety of them: supportive counseling, crisis counseling, educative counseling, and so forth.[1] Clinebell's text was revised in 1984, and while it includes a new theological rationale for the earlier project, it adds no new methods to those already in the earlier text.[2]

It is true that many pastoral counseling specialists have been using a variety of methods, including some not addressed in either edition of Clinebell's textbook. For most parish pastors, however, the techniques they employ in their pastoral care and counseling work have been, and remain, those described by Clinebell. Thus, for all the discussion currently taking place at more theoretical levels, we have seen virtually no innovation at the basic level of method and technique. If new winds are blowing in the field of pastoral theology, shouldn't more be happening at the basic level of methods? Shouldn't pastors be testing and refining new care and counseling techniques as they were in the 1960s? If such innovation is not taking place today at the grass roots, what will be the ultimate outcome of current theorizing? Will it prove to have been merely an academic exercise?

This book is a step toward addressing these questions. It argues for the addition of a single method to the techniques that are already available to parish pastors. It emphatically does not propose the elimination of any of the existing methods and is not offered as a replacement for any one. At the same time, I view it as a significant addition because it can be used in a variety of pastoral care and counseling contexts and with virtually any parishioner. Moreover, it reflects some of the new directions in pastoral theology, especially the effort to develop a biblically grounded approach to pastoral care and counseling. This method, while emerging out of recent developments in psychotherapy, has much affinity and compatibility with certain biblical forms, experiences, and ideas. Thus, in recommending it, I hope to contribute to the discussion in pastoral-theology circles of more adequate theological foundations for pastoral care and counseling. But I do so more from the level of method than the level of theory.

The method is "reframing," a technique widely used in psychotherapy over the past two decades. Reframing has been employed by many of the major therapists of our time, including Milton Erickson, Virginia Satir, Carl Whitaker, and Jay Haley. For the general reading public, Richard Bandler and John Grinder have made reframing readily accessible through their popular books.[3] In this book, I make particular use of the writings of Paul Watzlawick and his colleagues, John Weakland and Richard Fisch, primarily because their discussion of reframing is both philosophically sophisticated and extremely practical. Their book *Change: Principles of Problem Formation and Problem Resolution* is especially valuable because it treats reframing within the context of a philosophically based theory of change.[4] I am attracted to this approach to reframing because, as my earliest book on pastoral care attests, I consider change and how it is effected to be the fundamental issue of pastoral care and counseling.[5] In this writing, I have placed strong though not exclusive emphasis on the *Change* book, as an expression of the work that is being done at the Brief Therapy Center of the Mental Research Institute in Palo Alto, under the directorship of Fisch and Weakland.[6]

My goal is to draw attention to the reframing method and thereby make it available to the parish pastor. I have not written for the pastoral counseling specialist, who is probably already conversant with the reframing method, but for the parish pastor. My case illustrations are typical of the kinds that arise in the parish setting. I demonstrate through them *how* reframing works and *what* reframing requires of the pastor. I show that reframing makes a difference, often dramatic, in how such cases are handled and in their ultimate outcome. These examples show that the reframing method is genuinely, strikingly different from the other methods available to the parish pastor. "Reframing" is not just a new name for an already accepted and well-worn method. In fact, pastors accustomed to the tried-and-true methods developed in the 1950s and 1960s may find it startling and controversial. I welcome such reactions. The field of pastoral care and counseling has had little controversy, especially concerning its methods and techniques, in recent years. We desperately need the vigorous debate about methods that marked the field in its infancy.

This writing is a sequel to my earlier book, *Biblical Approaches to Pastoral Counseling,*[7] in which I explored the relationships between types of pastoral care (grief counseling, premarital counseling, and marriage counseling) and biblical forms or genres (psalms, proverbs, and parables). In the chapter on marriage counseling, I explored the counseling technique of *relabeling,* and showed that Jesus used a similar technique in his parables. This book, with its focus on reframing, expands on my earlier discussion: *reframing* is the method within which *relabeling* is one useful technique. I am now contending that the parabolic approach to pastoral counseling is appropriate for virtually every pastoral care and counseling situation, not just marriage counseling. Jesus' use of reframing through his parables is a central concern of this book; it enables us to locate the reframing method biblically, and provides insights for the reframing of contemporary pastoral care and counseling situations.

The parables, while fundamental to this study, are not the only biblical resource. I also make considerable use of the Book of Job because it illustrates the inadequacy of the current methods available to pastors for certain care and counseling situations, and the effectiveness of the reframing method in these instances. Using Clinebell's text and supporting literature, I suggest that the efforts of Job's three counselors can be viewed in the context provided by three well-established counseling methods. I also suggest that the experiences of Job's counselors reveal why these methods are likely to be ineffective at certain times. I then contend that God handled the situation effectively—employing the method of reframing. Thus, the case of Job illustrates how different methods—with different effects—may be used with the same individual. The case of Job also shows how, in some instances, the reframing method is more effective than any of the more traditional methods that are already available to the parish pastor, and that the deficiencies in these traditional methods are not due to their technical weaknesses, but to their theological assumptions, which raises some fundamental questions about the theological adequacy of such traditional procedures for certain cases encountered in parish-centered care and counseling.

In focusing on the Job case, I realize that the dialogues between Job and his counselors are poetic in form, so they are very different in structure and content from modern counseling. Also, we cannot assume that the only or even the primary objective of the counselors was to provide "pastoral care" for Job. Conversely, it would be ludicrous to claim that Eliphaz, Bildad, and Zophar were employing contemporary pastoral care and counseling methods as these are formulated in the pastoral care literature of today. Obviously, the three counselors were not conversant with these methods; their counseling is only a rough approximation of what a modern pastor would do in a similar situation. Hence, my point is neither that the Book of Job can be reduced to a modern counseling case nor that it demonstrates the bankruptcy of the traditional counseling methods of the 1950s and 1960s. I do believe, however, that the Book of Job enables us to identify potential theological weaknesses of these methods and thus to account for their ineffectiveness in certain situations, allowing us to see the theological reasons for needing and using reframing.

I do not expect that all pastors who read this book will be attracted to reframing. For those who are, the question arises: What type of pastor is attracted to the reframing method?

I contend that the method of reframing and the pastoral identity of the "wise fool" have a great deal in common. This term is from Alastair V. Campbell who identified three pastoral self-images—the shepherd, the wounded healer, and the wise fool. All three represent legitimate ways of being a pastoral care giver.[8] Yet, there is a rather strong affinity between the wise-fool image and the reframing method. The reframing method is tailor-made for the wise fool, and the wise-fool image will find greater acceptance as the reframing method is accorded a place among existing pastoral care and counseling methods. The pastoral image of the shepherd, once dominant, was especially congenial to the methods and techniques that first emerged in our field. It was joined in the 1970s by the wounded-healer type, which is suspicious of methods and techniques, favoring instead a ministry of "presence." Now, decades later, the wise fool is taking its place alongside the shepherd and wounded-healer images, and it is only natural that at least one pastoral care and counseling method suitable to this image would result. In this study I use the biblical figure Jonah to illustrate the affinities between the wise-fool image and the reframing technique.

A few words about the organization of this book are in order. Chapter 1 describes and illustrates the basic method of reframing, with specific focus on the theory of change formulated by Watzlawick, Weakland, and Fisch. Chapter 2 describes a number of counseling strategies and techniques employed in reframing. Chapter 3 provides a biblical basis for the reframing method by illustrating Jesus' use of reframing in his parables and healings. These three chapters set the stage for chapters 4 and 5, which involve two case illustrations: one concerning a young woman who is experiencing difficulty at work, and the other a teenage boy who is in conflict with his parents over his career and love interests. Together, these five chapters make an argument for the reframing method. Chapters 6 and 7 center on the case of Job. Chapter 6 concerns the three friends' efforts to counsel Job and links each one's approach to a contemporary method: Eliphaz and the method of supportive counseling, Bildad and the method of crisis counseling, and Zophar and the method of ethical, values, and meaning counseling. Chapter 7 focuses on God's response to Job. It demonstrates that God's effectiveness can be accounted for in part because God's response is an example of reframing. Chapter 8 concludes the study by exploring the affinities between the reframing method and the pastoral image of the wise fool.

PART 1

The Art
of Reframing

CHAPTER ONE
The Method
of Reframing

A house painter was standing on his ladder, absentmindedly brushing paint on the siding of a house. Suddenly, feeling movement on the ladder below, he looked down and saw a little girl on the third rung of the ladder; she was climbing toward him. His heart leaped into his throat as he realized her danger. One slight misstep and she would fall. His first instinct was to shout at her, telling her to go down. But would this frighten her and cause her to lose control? Would she fall between the rungs as she reversed course? Instead, he greeted her with a friendly hello and encouraged her to continue climbing. As she proceeded upward, he reached down to her until she was within his grasp. He caught her up in his arms and together they made their descent safely to the ground.

This is an example of reframing. The painter's initial instinct was to warn the little girl off the ladder. But, quickly considering the possible consequences of her attempt to reverse directions, especially if done against her desire to climb, he calculated that it was safer for her to continue upward. Thus he *reframed* the situation and, in doing so, violated his instinctive reaction. To encourage her to continue upward did not appear to make much sense, but, on reflection, it was the wiser course.

Reframings of this kind happen constantly. All of us have done them in our lives, perhaps many, many times. But we have not called them reframings. We have used other words—intuition, gut instinct, sudden inspiration, or whatever. Nor have we done them systematically. Our reframings have been random, occasional, and spur-of-the-moment.

Modern counseling theory has developed reframing into a method, making it intentional and self-conscious. The counselor cannot know in advance what the precise nature of the reframing will be—this will depend on what the counselee has to say—but he or she can know that it will be used. The counselor may also have some idea of when the reframing will be attempted and how it will be communicated to the counselee. Some counselors make a regular habit of planning and executing reframings, while others reframe on a more ad hoc basis. But what distinguishes reframings in the counseling setting from the ones we improvise in our own lives is that they are intentional, with specific, definable outcomes.

How do modern counselors understand reframing? In their book *Reframing,* Richard Bandler and John Grinder relate the following ancient Chinese Taoist story:

There was a farmer in a poor country village. He was considered very well-to-do because he owned a horse that he used for plowing and transportation. One day his horse ran away. All his neighbors exclaimed how terrible this was, but the farmer simply replied, "Maybe."

A few days later the horse returned and brought two wild horses with it. The neighbors all rejoiced at his good fortune, but the farmer simply replied, "Maybe."

The next day the farmer's son tried to ride one of the wild horses, but the horse threw him and broke the son's leg. The neighbors all offered their sympathy for his misfortune, but the farmer again replied, "Maybe."

The next week conscription officers came to the village to take young men for the army. They rejected the farmer's son because of his broken leg. When the neighbors told him how lucky he was, the farmer replied, "Maybe."

Bandler and Grinder use this story to show that the meaning any event has for us depends upon the *frame* in which we perceive it. When we change the frame, we change the meaning. Having two wild horses is a good thing until it is seen in the context of the son's broken leg. Then, the broken leg seems to be bad in the context of peaceful village life; but in the context of conscription and war, it suddenly becomes good. "This is called reframing: changing the frame in which a person perceives events in order to change the meaning. When the meaning changes, the person's responses and behaviors also change."[1]

As this story illustrates, reframing is not new. Bandler and Grinder note that "many fables and fairy tales include behaviors or events that change their meaning when the frames around them change."[2] The odd-looking chick appears to be an ugly duckling, but turns out to be a swan, more beautiful than the ducks to which the chick had compared himself. Jokes also involve reframings. Freud relates one of the "bath jokes" which treat rural Jews' aversion to taking baths: Two Jews met in the neighborhood of the bath-house. "Have you taken a bath?" asked one of them. "What?" asked the other in return, "Is there one missing?" This little joke involves a reframing made possible because the word *taken* has two very different meanings. In the questioner's intended frame, it means the act of bathing. In the answerer's frame, it means confiscating or stealing.[3]

This time-honored technique of reframing is now widely used in therapy: "When a therapist tries to get a client to 'think about things differently' or 'see a new point of view' or 'take other factors into consideration,' these are attempts to reframe events in order to get the client to respond differently to them."[4] Following is a typical example of a therapeutic reframing: A therapist is working with a family and the father says, "Nobody in this family has ever supported me by taking care of me. I always have to do it all myself. No one is ever solicitous or takes care of me, and it's been like this my whole life." To this lament, the therapist responds, "Thank God!" The father, of course, expected some kind of supporting comment like, "Oh, that's really too bad. Maybe we can make changes in the family." Instead, the therapist has forced the man to look at his complaint in a new light: the father has organized his life in such a way that no one in his family feels it necessary to take care of him—a very positive achievement.[5]

In this chapter, I present the method of reframing as formulated by Paul Watzlawick, John Weakland, and Richard Fisch in *Change: Principles of Problem Formation and Problem Resolution.*[6] This book has particular value because it provides a systematic formulation of the theory of change which undergirds the reframing method. It enables us to see how reframing differs in its objectives from every other pastoral care and counseling method in that it is designed to achieve a different kind of change.

The counseling theory presented in *Change* was developed at the Brief Therapy Center of the Mental Research Institute in Palo

Alto, California. The techniques of this center were explicitly designed for brief, and, therefore, problem-solving or problem-resolution counseling. Originally, they were considered most useful in situations where long-term counseling, with its emphasis on the clarification of complex interpersonal dynamics and the uncovering of unconscious motivations, was impractical. In time, however, the staff came to believe that their methods were inherently better than the methods of long-term counseling, a belief based in part on their counseling successes: their success rate was at least as good as that reported for long-term therapy. But it also had a philosophical rationale, for long-term counseling is based on a fallacy in human reasoning which the Center's counseling approach was designed to overcome: *the assumption that more of the same* is necessarily better than *less of the same.* The Palo Alto group challenges this common-sense belief.

FIRST-ORDER AND
SECOND-ORDER CHANGE

Watzlawick, Weakland, and Fisch propose that there are two kinds of change: *first-order change* that occurs within a given system which itself remains unchanged; and *second-order change* that alters the system itself. To illustrate the difference they cite the case of a person who is having a nightmare. This person can do many things *in* the dream—run, hide, fight, jump off a cliff—but no shift from any one of these behaviors to another would ever terminate the nightmare. This is first-order change. Second-order change involves a shift from dreaming to waking. Waking is not a part of the dream but a change to an altogether different state. Second-order change is a *change of change.* What occurs in second-order change is not merely a shift from stasis to change, but a fundamental alteration in change itself. In first-order change, the more things change, the more they remain the same. In second-order change, everything is different because the system itself is no longer the same.[7]

There are many situations in life in which first-order change is all that we require. When the temperature in the room falls to an uncomfortable level, we can adjust the thermostat until we are comfortable again. *More of the same* eventually achieves the desired effect. But in other situations of life, first-order change is insufficient. In these cases it may become the problem, making matters worse than they were before remedial efforts were tried. An illustration is the United States' experience with prohibiting the consumption of alcohol. At first, necessary restrictions were placed on alcohol consumption, but when these did not reduce the problem, *more of the same* was carried to its ultimate—the elimination of the problem through prohibition. Prohibition, however, turned out to be worse than the problem it was designed to eliminate: "Alcoholism rises, a whole clandestine industry comes into existence, the low quality of its products makes alcohol into even more of a public health problem, a special police force is needed to hunt down the bootleggers and in the process becomes unusually corrupt, etc., etc."[8]

A common approach to the reduction or elimination of a problem is to introduce its opposite as the logical solution. If a friend is depressed, we try to cheer her up. If our spouse is uncommunicative, perhaps even secretive, we try to get him to "open up." But these attempted solutions rarely, if ever, work. In fact, they increase the original problem and eventually become a problem in their own right. Efforts to get the husband to communicate make him more withholding and more secretive, even to the point where he refuses to make disclosures that are harmless and irrelevant, "just to teach her that she need not know everything." This behavior, in turn, adds further fuel to her worries: "If he refuses to talk to me about these little things, there *must* be something the matter." The less information he gives her, the more persistently she will seek it, and the more she seeks it, the less he will give her. In time, this very pattern of interaction becomes, itself, the problem. So, efforts to deal with a perceived problem by introducing its opposite result in a first-order change, where the more things change, the more they remain the same. What is required here is second-order change—an action that alters the interactional system itself.

THE MISHANDLING OF DIFFICULTIES

From this basic distinction between first- and second-order change, Watzlawick and his coauthors conclude that there are *difficulties* and there are *problems*. *Difficulties* are a fact of human existence. Some difficulties can be reduced or eliminated, while others are inescapable and have to be accepted as the price we pay for existing at all. Suffering, evil, and death are difficulties. Diseases, oppression, and poverty are problems. *Problems* are situations that are created and maintained through the mishandling of difficulties. There are basically three ways in which this mishandling can occur:

1. A difficulty exists for which action is necessary, but none is taken. This mishandling is called *simplification*. There are two forms of simplification. One is denial that a difficulty exists, often accompanied by an attack on those who disagree and who believe action should be initiated. The second is to acknowledge that there is a small difficulty, but to insist that it may be disposed of by a quick or simple solution. Such mishandling produces problems that not only fail to reduce or eliminate the difficulty but also have their own negative effects.

2. Change is attempted regarding a difficulty that, for all practical purposes, is either unchangeable or nonexistent. Here, action is taken when it should not be. This mishandling is called *utopianism*. It, too, can take one of two possible forms. The first is introjective utopianism, where we have deep, painful feelings of personal inadequacy for being unable to reach what are, in fact, unattainable goals (e.g., the goal of perfect happiness). Here, "the very act of setting this goal creates a situation in which the unattainability of the goal is not likely to be blamed on its utopian nature but rather on one's ineptitude: my life should be rich and rewarding, but I am living in banality and boredom; I should have intense feelings but cannot awaken them in myself."[9] Symptoms of this form of utopianism are depression, dropping out, withdrawal, suicidal thoughts, divorce, alienation, and nihilistic world views.

The second is projective utopianism. Its basic ingredient "is a moral, righteous stance based on the conviction of having found the truth and sustained by the resulting missionary responsibility of changing the world."[10] In this view, the failure to attain unattainable goals is not a negative reflection on us; the problem is with those who do not share our vision. Symptoms of this form of utopianism are righteous self-justification, paranoia, and the illusion of originality. The belief that we have the solution to difficulties that are actually unsolvable justifies hostile and uncivil attitudes toward others, causes us to become paranoid when others condemn or take our solution lightly, and leads us to entertain the false notion that this solution is new, that nothing of this sort has ever been attempted (and failed) in the past.

These two forms of utopianism are similar in one important respect: the premises on which they are based are considered to be more real or genuine than reality as we know it. Thus, the idea that we might attain perfect happiness or solve the unsolvable is more real to us than experiential evidence that these goals cannot be achieved.

The point is not that goals should not be set, worked toward, and realized. What the authors are challenging is the setting of unattainable goals, or envisioning change in difficulties that are, for all practical purposes, unchangeable. Unattainable goals do not reduce or eliminate difficulties. Instead, they create problems that did not previously exist. The failure to attain perfect happiness leads to feelings of inadequacy that would not have developed if the impossible goal had not been entertained. By setting goals that require actions by others that they are unlikely to perform, we create unnecessary and unproductive animosities between ourselves and others.

3. A first-order change is attempted in regard to a difficulty that can be changed only at the second-order level, or a second-order change is attempted when a first-order change would be appropriate. Action is taken at the wrong level—a mishandling called *paradox*. The attempted solutions are inherently paradoxical and incapable of producing second-order change. Instead, they imprison people in first-order change. When the paradoxical nature of these attempted solutions is revealed for what it is, a paradox, another paradox can be introduced that enables the desired second-order change to occur. In this case, the second paradox has practical or therapeutic effects. Thus, unrecognized or unacknowledged paradoxes usually effect only first-order change, while the self-conscious use of paradox achieves second-order change.

A mother was trying to change the behavior of her eight-year-old son, who did not like to do his homework. She told the therapist: "I want Andy to learn to do things, and I want him to do things—but I want *him* to want to do them. . . . I want him to *want* to do things, but I realize it's going to be something that we have to *teach* him."[11] Here, the mother has caught herself and her son in a paradox. She wants him to want to do things, that is, to want to do them *not* because she wants him to do them. This paradox is the classic double bind. The more she tries to *teach* her son to *want* to do things, the less he will perceive the doing of these things as something he *wants* to do. The more he does them, the more he does them because *she* wants him to do them. The desired change—from acting because *she* wants to acting because *he* wants—does not occur. The mother and son are locked into first-order change; the more things change, the more they remain the same.

Here are other examples of paradoxical communications: "I want you to dominate me." "Don't be so obedient." "Be spontaneous." "You should enjoy playing with the children, like other fathers do." "You know that you are free to go, and please don't worry if I start to cry." "Don't think about me at home alone tonight; just go out and have a good time."[12] A counseling session involves an unhappily married couple and their college-age son: The mother looks at her son with love and admiration and exclaims, "After all, it's a simple matter. All we want in the world is for George to have as happy a marriage as we have."[13] A husband who was challenging his wife's resistance to hiring household help explained, "I want her to be free enough to do what she wants."

A vast number of attempted solutions to difficulties are paradoxical and therefore place individuals in impossible dilemmas, binds, impasses, and deadlocks. They are damned if they do, and damned if they don't. First-order changes are achieved, but these only make for greater frustration and hopelessness. The son who would not do his homework now does it, but his mother knows that he does not want to do it, that he is doing it only because she is making him do it. Or, alternatively, he refuses to do his homework not just for the original reason (not wanting to do it) but also because he is now very aware that she wants him to do it. In either case, what began as the *difficulty* of unfinished homework has become a *problem* between mother and son: a mutually frustrating interpersonal conflict.

But paradox, when used with self-conscious intention, can also effect second-order change. Watzlawick's team develops this point in their theory of second-order change, which introduces the concept and method of reframing.

ACHIEVING SECOND-ORDER CHANGE
THROUGH REFRAMING

To reframe means to "change the conceptual and/or emotional setting or viewpoint in relation to which a situation is experienced and to place it in another frame which fits the 'facts' of the same concrete situation equally well or even better, and thereby changes its entire meaning."[14]

During one of the many nineteenth-century riots in Paris, the commander of an army detachment received orders to clear a city square by firing at the rabble. He commanded his soldiers to take up firing positions, their rifles leveled at the crowd. As a ghastly silence descended, he drew his sword and shouted at the top of his lungs: "Ladies and gentlemen, I have orders to fire at the rabble. But as I see a great number of honest, respectable citizens before me, I request that they leave so that I can safely shoot the rabble." The square was empty in a few minutes. What has happened here? Second-order change was achieved through reframing:

> The officer is faced with a threatening crowd. In typical first-order fashion he has instructions to oppose hostility with counter-hostility, with more of the same. Since his men are armed and the crowd is not, there is little doubt that "more of the same" will succeed. But in the wider context this change would not only be no change, it would further inflame the existing turmoil. Through his intervention the officer effects a second-order change—he takes the situation outside the frame that up to that moment contained both him and the crowd; he reframes it in a way acceptable to everyone involved, and with this reframing both the original threat and its threatened "solution" can safely be abandoned.[15]

The second-order change effected here has four identifiable features:

1. Second-order change is applied to what, in the first-order perspective, appears to be the solution. From the perspective of second-order change, this *solution* is the keystone of the problem itself. Instead of viewing the solution as genuine, an implementer of second-order change does something unexpected with it.

2. While first-order change always appears to be based on common sense—"If we demonstrate to the rioters our superior force, they will see the folly of their defiance"—second-order change usually appears odd, *un*commonsensical, unworkable, and impractical. Yet, by rejecting the obvious solution, declaring that it will only exacerbate the difficulty, we use paradox to shift the problem-solving process from a first-order to a second-order change. Here, paradox is used self-consciously and intentionally, whereas in first-order change, the paradoxical element is largely unreflective or unacknowledged, hidden under the guise of common sense.

3. Applying second-order change techniques to the proposed solution means that the difficulty is dealt with in the here and now. These techniques deal with effects, not their presumed causes. The crucial issue is *what* not *why.* While this approach may appear to be superficial, since the reasons for the difficulty are not explored, this is not really the case: "The solution of the problem of life is seen in the vanishing of this problem."[16] What could be deeper than this? Some people, of course, prefer to focus on the *whys* of their problems. This approach does not need to be discouraged entirely, but it can often result in an unnecessary and unproductive delay in dealing with the problem. So the objectives of second-order change are most likely to be achieved not by probing deeply into why the situation came to be the way it is, but by coming up with a means to overcome the present impasse, and eliminate the problem, once and for all.

4. The use of second-order change techniques lifts the situation out of the paradox-engendering trap created by the circularity of the attempted solution and places it in a different frame. The key to this shift from unwanted first-order change to the desired second-order change is the *reframing* of the situation.

Reframing challenges the assumption that the solution being employed *is* the solution, or *would be* the solution if only it could be performed better. Counselees often want counselors to help them do a better job of carrying out what they consider to be the "obvious" solution. But reframing challenges the idea that the perceived solution is appropriate. Usually, the therapist does not need to explain its deficiencies but proposes another approach. As this approach is based on a paradoxical reversal of the one which has been attempted, it usually makes little sense to the counselee. But, even as the counselee verbally resists this alternative, it has already begun to effect a change in the counselee's perception of the situation.

To illustrate the therapeutic use of the reframing method, Watzlawick and his colleagues relate the story of a young couple, Jerry and Sue, who requested marriage counseling because Sue was exasperated with Jerry's excessive dependence on his parents. Jerry agrees with Sue's assessment of the situation but says that he sees no way of solving it. All through his life, his parents have taken care of his every need and have showered him with all conceivable forms of support, but to reject their constant, unwanted help would be devastating to them, since constant giving is their idea of being good parents. His parents had chosen the couple's home and made the down payment, supplied most of the expensive furniture, and made all the landscaping and interior-decorating decisions. They make four, three-week visits each year during which they completely take over the house. Jerry's mother prepares all the meals, buys the groceries, washes everything in the house, and rearranges the furniture; his father cleans and services their two cars, rakes leaves, mows the lawn, plants, prunes, and weeds. When they go out to dinner or a show, his father pays all the expenses.

Jerry and Sue have tried various solutions. They have attempted to establish a minimum of independence, but even their mildest efforts are interpreted as a sign of ingratitude, which then provokes deep feelings of guilt in Jerry and impotent rage in Sue. These attempts also lead to ludicrous scenes in public, as when Jerry's mother and Sue each implore the supermarket cashier to accept her money, or when Jerry and his father literally fight over the check as soon as the waiter brings it to the table. To alleviate some of their feelings of indebtedness, Jerry and Sue have sent his parents an expensive gift after each visit, only to receive a still more expensive gift in return. The harder they try to gain their independence, the more his parents try to "help" them, and all four are caught in a typical *more of the same* impasse. The attempted solutions have only compounded the problems for Jerry and Sue.

From the information provided, it was clear to the counselor that any successful intervention had to be carried out within the only context the parents could understand, namely, the overriding importance to them of being good parents. Since one of their quarterly visits was imminent, Jerry and Sue were instructed by the counselor to do the following: They were to stop cleaning the house several days before the visit, to permit the dirty laundry to accumulate, to stop washing the cars and to leave their gas tanks nearly empty, to neglect the garden, and to deplete the kitchen of almost all groceries. They were to make no effort to prevent his parents from paying for the groceries, gasoline, and entertainment, but were to wait calmly until this was done. Sue was to leave dirty dishes in the kitchen and expect Jerry's mother to wash them. Jerry was to read or watch television while his father worked in the garden and garage. From time to time he was to stick his head out the door, check his father's progress, and ask cheerfully, "Hi, Dad, how's it going?" He and Sue were not to make any attempts to get Jerry's parents to acknowledge that they had a right to their own independence. They were to accept everything done for them as a matter of course and to thank Jerry's parents perfunctorily.

The result was dramatic. Jerry's mother and father cut their visit short. Before leaving, Dad took Jerry aside and told him that he and Sue were much too pampered, that they had become too accustomed to being supported and waited on, and that it was time for them to begin behaving like adults. Jerry's parents' determination to be "good parents" had not been attacked or undermined, but it was clear that good parenting no longer meant overindulging Jerry and Sue, but dedicating themselves to the equally gratifying parental task of enabling their son and his wife to gain their own independence.

In this case, the therapeutic intervention by the counselor was the proposal of an alternative solution. This proposal achieved a reframing of the situation, and was self-consciously paradoxical. The way for Jerry and Sue to free themselves of their dependent and submissive relationship was not to continue to resist it but to invite and encourage it. Because this alternative was paradoxical, a conceptual and emotional reframing occurred even before the relationship itself had changed. That the objective situation was subsequently altered is, of course, not to be minimized. Had Jerry's parents not reacted as they did, it is likely that Jerry and Sue would have reverted to their original assessment of the difficulty: they had a "marital problem." But the actual reframing occurred before the condition itself was changed, as the counselor took the couple's own attempted solutions and reversed them, in paradoxical fashion, creating a very different scenario for addressing the difficulty.

Jerry and Sue had come for counseling because Sue could no longer endure Jerry's excessive dependence on his parents. The therapist's proposal did not directly address her questions: "Will my husband ever change?" "Can you get him to change?" Instead, he reframed the issue by focusing on Jerry's parents' genuine desire to be "good parents." This was a refocusing of the difficulty. The *why* questions—"Why does he need this dependency?" and "Why can't he free himself from it?"—were not addressed at all. "What" took the place of "why."

The authors of *Change* cite other examples of the therapeutic use of reframing: A man who worries that his fear and anxiety over public speaking will be noticeable to the audience is instructed to tell the audience at the outset how very afraid he is. A dental assistant who worries that she will make a mistake, causing her boss to fire her, is instructed to commit one small but rather stupid mistake every day on purpose. A young man who has very grandiose ideas for his life is not "helped" to scale them down to size, but gently criticized for setting his sights "too low" and for not being "ambitious enough." The parents of a teenage son who stays out beyond his curfew are instructed to abandon their attempted solution (i.e., punitive sanctions) and instead, to lock the door, turn out the lights, and go to bed before he comes home. When he knocks, they are to take their time getting to the door and ask innocently, "Who's there?" They are to apologize for making him wait in the cold, and then stumble back to bed without the usual interrogation about where he has been and why he is so late. These alternative solutions are based on the paradox of doing the precise opposite of what has been tried already, and what common sense would have dictated.

FOUR STEPS TO CHANGE

From this discussion of second-order change through reframing, Watzlawick's team recommends a simple four-step procedure in approaching any difficulty or problem:

1. Define the difficulty or problem in concrete terms.

2. Investigate the solutions attempted so far.
3. Define clearly the concrete change to be achieved.
4. Formulate and implement a plan to produce this change.

Step 1. In the first step, it is important to distinguish between difficulties that have a solution and those that, for all practical purposes, do not. The problem-solving method developed by Watzlawick and his associates does not apply to difficulties for which there is no cure or known relief, such as the death of a loved one. But these insoluble difficulties can be redefined in terms of "How can I learn to live with it?" Thus, the goal is to define a difficulty or a problem in such a way as to insure that it has one or more potential solutions.

Step 2. The investigation of solutions attempted so far is especially crucial because the formulation and implementation of a plan to produce the change will involve a reversal of the previously tried solutions. "A careful exploration of these attempted solutions not only shows what kind of change must *not* be attempted, but also reveals what maintains the situation that is to be changed and where, therefore, change has to be applied."[17]

Step 3. Clear definition of the change to be achieved is a safeguard against getting caught up in wrong solutions and compounding rather than resolving the difficulty. The authors warn that an ineffective reframing occurs when the existing difficulty is considered so complex and deep-seated that only complicated and extensive procedures hold any promise of producing change. The counselee may contribute to this sense of complexity by stating the desired change in seemingly meaningful but actually useless terms: Mark wants to be happier or communicate better with his wife. Millie wants to get more out of life. Anne wants to worry less. A specific and concrete change needs to be agreed upon, even though others may seem to have equal merit. A change that is achievable breaks the pattern of frustration caused by attempted solutions that have not produced the desired results.

Step 4. The plan devised to effect the desired change needs to fit the specific case. Every situation is unique so every plan must also be unique. Reframing plans cannot be mass produced. Normally, they require imagination, playfulness, and recognition that the counselor may appear foolish or even frivolous to the counselee because paradox plays as important a role in the problem resolution as it played in the problem formation. On the other hand, although imagination and playfulness are often required in devising the plan, their use does not give counselors license to propose any idea that comes to mind. The imagination involved is controlled and disciplined; the plan is specific to the situation, takes account of previous attempts to solve the difficulty, and embraces all the relevant facts.

The authors of *Change* note that their own counseling failures have resulted either from setting an unrealistic or inappropriate goal for change, or from encountering difficulty in motivating the counselee to carry out the proposed plan. Some counselees "forget" to follow it or, considering it silly or useless, simply refuse. Desperation is insufficient motivation for enacting the proposed plan. Counselees need to believe that a plan which seems foolish actually makes a great deal of sense. When they perceive this, they usually follow the counselor's suggestion. In most cases, the counselor does not expect the plan to be implemented in every detail. Counselees are expected and, at times, encouraged to improvise. However, improvisations that change the essence of the plan are discouraged because this is tantamount to sabotaging the therapeutic process itself.

CONCLUSION

In focusing on the Brief Therapy Center's approach to reframing, we have been concerned with a therapeutic method which emphasizes *the reframing plan*. Not all psychotherapists who use the reframing method insist on the formulation of a reframing plan in every instance. We should not assume that all situations in which reframing is indicated in pastoral care and counseling will require a formal plan. On the one hand, reframing may be used more incidentally. On the other hand, pastors will often find it appropriate to devise a reframing plan similar to those developed by the Brief Therapy Center team. It is true that pastors are not accustomed to being so directive in their counseling work, a condition partly attributable to the client-centered or "non-directive" nature of much care and counseling even today—which leaves much initiative to the counselee. While I am deeply grateful for the client-centered approach, I am also convinced that pastors should seize more initiative in their care and counseling work. The reframing method supports such initiative taking.[18]

Of course, there is always the danger that a method like reframing may be abused by overenthusiastic or irresponsible ministers. The following warning by Bandler and Grinder must be taken very seriously:

> Reframes are not con-jobs. What makes a reframe work is that it adheres to the well-formedness conditions of a particular person's needs. It's not a deceptive device. It's actually accurate. The best reframes are ones which are *as* valid a way of looking at the world as the way the person sees things now. Reframes don't necessarily need to be more valid, but they really can't be less valid.[19]

Thus, if a father complains that his daughter has never married because she is "just too stubborn," the counselor, knowing something of the reasons she is still unmarried, may observe, "Aren't you proud that she can say 'no' to men with bad intentions?" This "reframe" is a thoroughly valid way of looking at the situation. Although a simple suggestion, it might help the father see his daughter from a perspective that would allow him to be proud of her—one that would not have occurred to him without the shift in viewpoint offered by the counselor.[20] The reframing, whether a brief comment like this or a more elaborate plan, must be a valid way of looking at a situation, taking all known facts into account.

The reframing must be appropriate for the particular individual. Saying to this father, "You should like your daughter's stubbornness because it means she's a liberated woman," probably will not work with him. One must find a set of perceptions appropriate to the particular person's model of the world.[21] If the counselee rejects a proposed reframing, his behavior does not necessarily mean he is resistant to looking at the situation from a different point of view. It could indicate that the counselor has not yet found an alternative perspective that is valid for this person.

In short, reframing is not a science but an art. Moreover, it is a hopeful art. It builds on the idea that a person can break out of limiting preconceptions to a broader understanding of human possibilities. In observing that reframing shifts the client's framework from a negative to a positive one, Stephen and Carol Lankton note that it achieves one or more of the following goals:

1. It identifies the motives, needs, desires, or intentions of current or past behavior and labels these *positive* (i.e., well-intentioned under the circumstances).

2. It discriminates between the motive and the self-defeating behaviors so that new and more effective means to satisfy the actual needs of the client can be developed.

3. It restructures the experience so that new learnings and desirable experiences are created in place of the problematic behaviors, feelings, and thoughts.

The Lanktons add that "reframing is especially useful for treating clients who have problems they consider to be out of their control." This, they wryly note, "includes most clients."[22] We might add, "and most parishioners too."

CHAPTER TWO
The Techniques of Reframing

To perform a task well, we need to know certain techniques and to be able to use them with some facility. Ballet dancers, courtroom lawyers, automobile mechanics, seamstresses, poets, and research scientists all use techniques in the performance of their work. In some cases, they have been using them for so long that these actions have become second nature. They may not even think of them as techniques anymore. These individuals might have difficulty explaining what they do to someone else, say, someone who is just learning the job. In other cases, a technique may be so new to us, or us to it, that our use of it seems unnatural, forced, and contrived. When we use it, we feel uncomfortable and ill-at-ease, and we become so preoccupied with the method that we almost forget the purpose or goal behind it.

Yet, whether we are comfortable or uncomfortable with certain techniques, we know that they are indispensable to the accomplishment of tasks. Since pastoral care and counseling is a task, it too involves the use of techniques, and our effectiveness as caregivers will depend, in part, on how skilled we are in our use of them.

Over the years, a number of techniques have been developed in support of the reframing method. Like all skills, they can, and have, been abused. But when used responsibly, they can make the difference between successful and unsuccessful reframing. In this chapter, I will describe a number of these techniques and illustrate, through case materials and pastoral applications, their typical or potential use.

PARADOXICAL INTENTION

The use of paradox is especially helpful in therapy for phobias, compulsions, and unwanted behavior patterns that are triggered by certain situations. This technique involves encouraging or instructing clients to wish to bring about the very thing they fear will happen. When they wish for it to happen, they discover that it does not happen because the wishing and the fearing are two opposites that cancel each other out.[1] Here is an illustration of the technique of paradoxical intention:

A teenage apprentice is called to his boss's office. Because of the excitement, or even because the room is warm, he perspires and the boss makes a harmless remark about it. The next time the apprentice is called to the boss's office, he worries that he may perspire again. He carefully wipes his face and enters the office, and the fear of perspiring drives the sweat from his pores. After the second experience he is certain that the third time he faces the boss, he will be dripping with sweat. And, sure enough, he is. Now he tries to run away from the situation. He avoids the boss's office; he calls in sick when he expects to be summoned, takes tranquilizers, and gets trapped more and more in a desperate cycle. His anxiety spreads to other situations. He fears that he may sweat when talking to any adult, so he withdraws. He becomes a loner, his shyness increases, and he finds less courage to face people. His boss is now on the verge of firing him because he cannot use an apprentice who is sick so often. Finally, in desperation, the boy seeks professional help.

The therapeutic intervention involved encouraging the boy to intend exactly what he feared, namely, sweating. Through patient coaching from the therapist, he learned to tell himself that he would show his boss just how much he *could* sweat. He would perspire a puddle in the room so the boss could swim away in it! It occurred to him that this would be a good way for him to get rid of the boss! The next time he was called in to see the boss, he was unable to sweat. The wish to sweat and the fear of sweating canceled each other out.[2]

In another case, a client would never go near a bus stop because she feared that she would push someone in front of the bus. The psychotherapist took the client to the bus stop and, as a bus approached, told the client, "Push me in front of the bus. Go ahead. Do it!" The client not only did *not* do what she was told to do, but also realized that the feared event would never take place, even if she discontinued her compulsive behavior (avoidance of the bus stop).[3]

In still another case, a middle-aged, unmarried man was leading an isolated life due to agoraphobia, or fear of being in open or public places. As time passed, his anxiety-free territory progressively diminished. Eventually his fear not only prevented him from going to work, but threatened to cut him off even from visiting the neighborhood stores on which he depended for food and other basic necessities. In his desperation, he decided to commit suicide. He planned to get into his car and drive in the direction of a mountain top about fifty miles from his home. He was convinced that after driving a few city blocks his anxiety would produce a heart attack, which would put him out of his misery. Instead, he arrived safely at his destination and, for the first time in many years, he found himself free from anxiety. While this cure was not the work of a trained therapist, it illustrates the technique of paradoxical intention. By going out in public for the purpose of killing himself, the man discovered that public places produced no fear in him.[4]

There are limitations to this technique. Some individuals are better suited for paradoxical intention than others. It is especially helpful for the client to have a sense of humor which enables him or her to achieve the self-distancing necessary to do what the therapist encourages or instructs. Clients who are poorly suited for this technique are "yes, but" types who find something wrong with the proposed reframing or feel ridiculed or offended when the therapist offers a paradoxical formulation. This strategy is also inappropriate for very depressed persons because the paradoxical formulation may appear to be a mockery of their condition. Instructing a person who is depressed to experience deeper levels of depression is cruel. On the other hand, paradoxical intention may be useful in cases of acute grief, as when a therapist asks a bereaved husband whether he would want his wife back, even for a little while, if this would mean that she would have to go through her painful death all over again?

Paradoxical intention is especially appropriate when used by pastors in pastoral work with individuals and families, but it may also help to deal with fears, compulsions, and unwanted behavior at the congregational level. For example, at an elders' meeting, there was general consensus among the elders present that the congregation was unfriendly to visitors. They agreed that they needed to be more friendly themselves, and admitted to feeling guilty for not talking to visitors as much as they should. The pastor had heard such discussions many times before and knew they rarely had much effect. So he made the following radical request: "For the next few Sundays, I want you to go out of your way to avoid our visitors. If you find yourselves tempted to greet one of them, restrain yourselves. And if they approach you, I want you to turn away and talk, instead, to a friend. Then, at our next elders' meeting, I'll ask each of you to report on how successful you were in avoiding the visitors." When asked why he would want the elders to behave this way, the pastor explained that he could handle the task of greeting visitors himself and that most of them want to maintain their anonymity anyway. These were arguments that he had actually heard voiced by some parishioners. While he, of course, did not agree with this reasoning, it provided a plausible rationale for his instructions. Some elders remained puzzled about the pastor's request, some felt it was a trick, but all agreed to follow his instructions. At the next elders' meeting, there was a discussion of their success in avoiding the visitors. Not all had violated the pastor's instructions, but many had. Overall, however, they had a very different discussion than would have taken place if each elder had been asked to report on his or her efforts to make contact with visitors. The conversation was much more alive and spirited, and there was none of the negative self-recrimination which had characterized their earlier discussions of the issue.

DEREFLECTION

Self-examination leads to healthy self-assessment, but exaggerated self-observation may be harmful. To counteract hyper-reflection, one cannot simply counsel clients not to think so much about a certain subject; this advice simply draws their attention to what they are trying to avoid. It is equally difficult not to think about anything at all. The technique of dereflection involves suggesting that clients think of something else, thus detaching them from their symptoms and directing them to another, more positive subject. In most cases, clients are asked to think of desirable, positive, and healthy activities that would enrich their lives, and to select one of these activities every time they are likely to hyper-reflect, thereby discovering for themselves which alternative activities work best in distracting them from their negative ruminations.[5] Here is a typical case in which the technique of dereflection was employed:

An intelligent high-school student should easily have passed his tests, but he worried so much about forgetting everything that he actually performed very poorly. He also began to develop psychosomatic stomach disorders that worsened as test times drew close. Finally, his parents, concerned about his poor grades in school and his stomach problems, which contributed to absenteeism, sought professional help. The therapist instructed the student and his parents to avoid the subject of school for three months. Instead, he was encouraged to become involved in extracurricular activities, to read anything he wanted to read, and to have a good time on weekends. Skeptical at first, the parents cooperated. Whenever he began to talk about school, they asked him about choir practice, his soccer games, or his weekend plans. Within six months, his grades had improved from a C to an A- average.

This technique can also be used in counseling with couples who are engaged in exaggerated evaluation and assessment of their relationship together. No doubt, most married couples are not reflective enough about their relationship together. But there are some couples who are constantly analyzing their relationship, and making themselves miserable in the process. These couples are excellent candidates for dereflection. When Johnny Carson, host of the *Tonight Show,* asked Steve Lawrence and Eydie Gorme why their marriage had survived so long, Eydie replied, "Because we have never had a meaningful conversation together!" This, of course, could not be literally true, but it makes the point that marriages can suffer from too much as well as too little reflection on the relationship itself. Pastors may also find that dereflection works with a congregation that engages in exaggerated negative reflection on itself, or is continually obsessed about some negative experience in its past (e.g., the suicide of a previous pastor). When such talk begins to emerge, it should not be cut off with a comment like "Let's not be so negative about ourselves." Instead, the members should be instructed to think of something very positive about the congregation. As a way to solidify this dereflection strategy, one pastor had the congregation develop a brochure in which its strengths were listed and described. Of course, pastors need to be aware of the danger that they will use the dereflection technique to support a Pollyanna-like attitude toward the congregation and their own ministry. Usually, though, one can readily discern the difference between healthy self-reflection and exaggerated self-examination. The one is a stimulus to growth while the other makes for stagnation and inertia.

CONFUSION

The confusion technique, formulated by Milton Erickson, is illustrated by the following event:

One windy day a man came rushing around the corner of a building and bumped hard against Erickson, who was bracing himself against the wind. Erickson, who had been partially paralyzed by polio when he was seventeen, nonetheless managed to keep his balance. Before the man could utter an apology, Erickson glanced at his watch and stated, courteously, as if the man had inquired the time of day, "It's exactly ten minutes of two," though it was actually closer to four, and walked on. About a half block away, Erickson turned and saw the man looking at him, undoubtedly still puzzled and bewildered by Erickson's words. This odd remark of Erickson's had redefined the context from one in which apology was anticipated to one that would have been appropriate if the other man had asked the time of day. But even this was bewildering because of the patent inaccuracy of the information in contrast to the courteous manner in which it was given. Thus, a therapist may preface an especially important intervention (e.g., interpretation, observation, advice, or instruction) with a deliberately confusing statement. Unnerved by the confusing statement, the client will be more likely to respond positively to the therapist's following statement.[6] Here is an illustration of the therapeutic use of the confusion technique:

A therapist believes that her client's problem can be resolved only if he will initiate a discussion with his boss. She is also fairly certain, however, that the client will advance many reasons as to why talking with his boss will be counterproductive. She bases this judgment, in large part, on her observation that he has been a "yes, but" counselee through much of the counseling process. To ensure that he will at least give serious consideration to her suggestion, she prefaces it with a superficially erudite but actually opaque statement about human nature. Caught off guard by the discrepancy between her first and second statements, he responds positively to the second, accepting her recommendation that he talk with his boss.

The confusion technique is also useful when the therapist perceives that it would be beneficial to the client to have to depend on his own problem-solving skills, and to struggle through to his own interpretation and resolution of the problem. Thus, the same therapist, working with another client, responded to his questions concerning what he should do about a particular problem by making a series of confusingly imprecise and virtually incoherent comments. After each of the therapist's remarks, the client moved on his own toward clarification of the problem and what he might do to resolve it. In effect, the therapist had reversed the usual pattern in which the client is confused and incoherent and the counselor ensures that the process is rational and clear.

Obviously, the confusion technique is not easy to use. While we often make confusing remarks unintentionally, it is difficult to do so on purpose. It is also hard to resist the urge to clarify a confusing statement when faced with the puzzlement of the client. But the strategic value of confusing language should not be overlooked or minimized. The confusion technique may be used, for example, to ensure that the pastor's views on a particular issue will be taken seriously by a decision-making group. Members of the committee may be so unnerved after listening to a particularly incoherent statement from their pastor that they will be anxious to respond positively to what the pastor says next. An arcane or hopelessly involved theological statement can be an especially valuable means of creating such confusion. Also effective is a statement which is obviously false, such as Erickson's words, "It's exactly ten minutes of two." A rambling and pointless psychological, sociological, or historical allusion may also serve the purpose. Pastors who are reluctant or unable to make confusing statements deliberately may choose to wait until a committee member has done so, and then immediately offer their views, clearly and concisely, on the subject at hand. It will be met with relief and approval.

ADVERTISING INSTEAD OF CONCEALING

There are many problems whose common denominator is some kind of socially inhibiting or embarrassing handicap—either something the person cannot help doing but should not be doing, or something he or she would like to do but cannot. Many people attempt to deal with this problem through control and concealment, but the harder they try to hide their inhibition or hardship, the more immobilizing it becomes. Thus, the advertising technique amounts to a complete reversal of the solution attempted thus far. Instead of trying to conceal the symptom, the client makes it known. Because the attempted solution (concealment) *is* the problem, the problem disappears when the solution is abandoned.

Fear of public speaking is an excellent example of an inhibition which can be addressed with the advertising technique. This fear is the greatest one of all for many people. We are afraid that our tension will become obvious and overwhelm us in front of the audience. Efforts to hide the shaking of our hands and the tremor in our voices only cause us to become more tense. The solution is to reveal to the audience what we have attempted to conceal, by confessing, "I'm awfully nervous up here in front of all of you." This confession reduces the tension as the audience nods sympathetically and makes allowances for the speaker's fears. Also, it often prompts the audience to place a higher value on the content of the address, as they are likely to be impressed that the speaker was able to deliver the speech at all![7]

The most obvious uses of the advertising technique by pastors are those in which the socially inhibiting or embarrassing handicap is the pastor's own. There are many times in pastoral ministry where concealment of weaknesses or handicaps is attempted, and the result is greater immobilization. The pastor has anxieties and fears about pastoral visitation in the hospital, about meeting with the family after the death of a family member, about conducting a series of premarital sessions, or about confronting a parishioner whose behavior is having a negative effect on congregational morale. Revealing these anxieties and fears in appropriate ways often helps to reduce their effect on the pastor and often prompts hearers to make similar revelations about themselves. But care must be taken that such revelations do not become so habitual and routine that the audience hears them as excuses for poor performance, or as manipulative efforts to win their sympathy.

THE BELLOC PLOY

People often get involved in self-perpetuating interpersonal tangles, in which ugliness in one person engenders ugliness in the other, and then feeds back on itself. The Belloc Ploy, named after Jean Giraudoux's play *L'Apollon de Belloc,* involves instructing the client to make a flattering statement to the person with whom he has been having conflicts. The client usually resists this suggestion at first, but as he considers how it might play, he becomes intrigued; the more he thinks about it, the funnier it seems: "Imagine me telling that clown that I like the way he presents his ideas in our case conferences!" Often the atmosphere between the two combatants changes even if the behavioral prescription is never carried out. The intention to make the flattering remark effects a subtle change in the client's demeanor; this change is noticed by his adversary, who responds, however subtly, in kind.

An experienced, intelligent executive assistant was having difficulties with one of her bosses. Made to feel insecure by her independent and rather forceful manner, he missed few opportunities to degrade her in front of other employees. She felt so offended by this behavior that she adopted an even more distant and condescending attitude toward him, to which he reacted with more of the belittling remarks that had made her angry in the first place. As the situation escalated, he was about to recommend her transfer or dismissal, and she was considering quitting her job. Instead, she sought professional help. The therapist instructed her to wait for the next incident and then take her boss aside and tell him with an obvious show of embarrassment, "I have wanted to tell you for a long time, but I didn't know how—It's a crazy thing, but when you treat me like you just did, it really turns me on. I don't know why—maybe it has something to do with my father." She was then to leave the room quickly before he could respond.

At first horrified, and then intrigued, she finally found the whole idea enormously funny and was anxious to try it. When she came back for her next appointment, however, she stated that her boss's behavior had somehow changed overnight and that he had been polite and easy to get along with ever since. Clearly, her knowledge that she could deal differently with the situation brought about a subtle change in her behavior that directly affected the interpersonal reality. There is no other plausible explanation for her boss's sudden change toward her.[8]

The Belloc Ploy can be a valuable technique in reducing and eliminating interpersonal conflicts between members of the congregation. Pastors are frequently pressured to take sides in a personality conflict between two members. Not wanting to be drawn into a "no win" situation, pastors usually respond with noncommittal remarks: "I can see your point," or "I can see why you would feel the way you do about Ruth." These comments, however, usually leave the complainant dissatisfied. She may wish she had not mentioned the problem to the pastor, and may feel that the pastor thinks less of her because of her criticism of Ruth. The Belloc Ploy offers the pastor a genuine alternative. When a parishioner complains to the pastor about another member, the pastor can listen to the complaint and then suggest that the parishioner say something to Ruth that is no less outrageous than the statement the executive assistant was to make to her boss. The next time Ruth makes a cutting remark, Eleanor is instructed to make a statement similar to the following: "Knowing how much we mean to each other, what you just said, while it was a little critical, came across as so affirming and so supportive." Even if Eleanor never actually says these words to Ruth, the change in Eleanor, as she realizes that she can deal with the situation differently, should result in a change in the interpersonal reality itself. Moreover, Eleanor will feel that she has been heard by the pastor, for he has confirmed, indirectly, that he believes Ruth has in fact been unloving toward Eleanor.

WHY SHOULD YOU CHANGE?

Counselors often find that their clients resist their efforts, behaving as if they want to defeat the expert and thereby prove that the problem cannot be solved. Their call for help leads to common-sense advice from counselors, to which they respond with reasons showing that the advice will not work. In the "Why Should You Change?" technique, the therapist leaves the frame dictated by common sense and asks the apparently absurd question, "Why should you change?" The client is ill-prepared for this question; according to the rules of his game, it is simply assumed that he *should* change. This question therefore creates a new game, one the client no longer controls. A variant form of this technique is the question, "How could you possibly change?" Here, the therapist finds the very idea of change incredible. Why would you, in your position, do anything differently? Another variant is to inform the client that any change that might occur in his condition will necessarily be very slow, and that under no circumstances, for the time being, should he let his plans go beyond the thinking stage. This technique typically energizes a resistant client to prove the therapist wrong, and, in this way, moves the therapeutic process beyond its present impasse. Here is an illustration of this technique:

A teenage boy had been suspended from school after he was caught selling barbiturates on the campus. Kevin was annoyed, not because he would be missing school, but because his business would be interrupted. His annoyance became intense anger when the school principal told him the suspension was for his own good and was intended to help him. Mr. Green then informed Kevin that, during the period of his suspension, he would be given credit for any school work he did at home, and that his mother would be allowed to pick up his assignments from school. Kevin had always been a poor student; furious with Mr. Green over the suspension, he told his mother that under no circumstances would he do any school work. She sought help from the therapist, hoping that he could influence Kevin to accept Mr. Green's ruling and therefore not remain so angry and intransigent about the school work. Instead, realizing that Kevin's anger at Mr. Green afforded a lever for change, the therapist took another approach. Kevin's mother was instructed to tell him that she had come to realize something she probably should not reveal to Kevin, but would do so anyway: Since Mr. Green believed that a student could not keep up with class work unless he or she attended school faithfully, she was quite certain he had suspended Kevin to make him fail the entire school year. So, if Kevin were to do his school work as well or even better on his own than when he attended class, Mr. Green would be embarrassed. It might be best, therefore, if Kevin did not do too well.

When Kevin heard this, his face lit up with a diabolical grin and revenge shone in his eyes. In a follow-up session, his mother reported that he had thrown himself into the school work and was getting better grades than ever before.[9]

Pastors are often confronted with parishioners' unexplainable resistance to change that they would normally be expected to desire and support.[10] Reasoning with such persons is usually futile; they can always produce a counterargument for why change is undesirable or impossible. The "Why Should You Change?" technique is especially suited for these clients. When the parishioner expresses reasons to explain why circumstances should remain as they are, the pastor may simply agree and say that there is no reason they should change. If the pastor was the one who originally proposed changes, only to be met with counterarguments, she may praise or congratulate the parishioner for making such a convincing case that she, herself, has changed her mind. This strategy forces the resistant parishioner to participate in a new game for which he is ill-prepared, and for which his own resistant maneuvers are ineffective.

BENEVOLENT SABOTAGE

The technique of benevolent sabotage is especially useful when one person is ineffectively struggling to exert some influence or control over another's behavior. Both persons know that the one is in no position to demand compliance from the other. The technique of benevolent sabotage involves taking a *one-down,* as opposed to *one-up* position, based on a frank admission that one is unable to control the other's behavior. With this admission, the other quickly finds that assertion and defiance do not make much sense and becomes more willing to be cooperative. Here is an example of the technique of benevolent sabotage:

The parents of a high-school boy have realized that their threats against him do no good. They have tried various sanctions to no avail. Finally, they seek professional help. They are instructed by the therapist to say to him: "We want you home by 11 P.M.—but if you are not, there is nothing we can do." With this frank admission of powerlessness, the parents reframe the situation from one in which their authority is being challenged to one in which defiance makes little sense. To show they mean what they say, the parents are instructed to go to bed at eleven o'clock and pretend that they are asleep when Tim eventually returns home. The following morning they are not to discuss the time he finally arrived home unless he mentions it himself. If he does so, they are to repeat what they said the previous evening: "If you are not home by eleven, there is really nothing we can do about it." Their tone is to be that of cheerful resignation to the inevitable, not one of sarcasm or frustration.[11]

The key element in this technique is that the desired behavior or response is clearly stated: "We want you home by eleven." This is clear and unambiguous. No less ambiguous is the frank admission that the speaker cannot force compliance, knows this, and knows that the other person knows it. This technique can be especially useful with parishioners whose open defiance of the congregation's programs and goals is having a deleterious effect on the spirit of the congregation, particularly in cases in which the pastor has already attempted to placate, cajole, warn, or even threaten them. By telling them, "This is what I would like for you to do," and then specifying the desired behavior, the pastor gives a clear and unambiguous signal as to what she wants from them. This way, there can be no doubt of the desired compliance, and no doubt, on either side, of whether it has occurred. However, by informing these individuals that there is nothing she can do if they fail to cooperate, the pastor gives an equally clear signal that she knows she cannot force compliance, and knows that they know this, too. American churches are best understood as voluntary associations in which individuals may choose to participate and, for the most part, are free to decide the degree to which they will participate and be cooperative and supportive. By admitting that there is nothing she can do if they do not comply, the pastor takes a *one-down* position, but only after stating clearly what she would consider cooperative behavior to be. For this technique to be effective, it is important that the pastor's demeanor be one of cheerful resignation—genuinely so—and not of sarcasm or frustration. She cheerfully accepts the fact that certain parishioners may continue to be recalcitrant, defiant, and uncooperative. Yet, she indicates to them: "I can live with it. Indeed, I'm doing quite well without your support." If they do change, however, it is appropriate for the pastor to acknowledge this, usually with a simple expression of thanks. If she makes too much of the change (i.e., becomes effusive in her appreciation), the members may feel they were manipulated into compliance and become defiant again.

THE ILLUSION OF ALTERNATIVES

The illusion of alternatives is a useful technique in situations where one person wants another person to act in a certain way, but senses that the other is resisting. Instead of cajoling and threatening, which only makes the other person more stubborn and defiant, one presents the other with a choice which excludes the possibility of doing nothing at all: "Do you want to go to bed at 7:45 or at 8 P.M.?" Here, one creates the illusion that the other has an alternative. Going to bed is the desired outcome. The choice offered to the other does not include deciding whether to go or not to go to bed. It merely offers flexibility as to when this outcome will be accomplished.

A variation on the technique involves offering a choice between two behaviors, either of which will facilitate a third outcome: "Do you wish to take a bath before going to bed or would you rather put your pajamas on in the bathroom?" Here, the questioner's concern is to get the child to go to bed voluntarily. Since either action—taking a bath or putting on his pajamas—will facilitate this outcome, the questioner does not especially care which course of action is chosen. In this case, as in the previous one, a specific frame is created that excludes the undesirable outcome—the failure to go to bed in a reasonably timely fashion.[12]

The illusion of alternatives is often used by family members to maintain control over other members. A mother buys two shirts, a blue one and a brown one, for her son. The next day, he appears wearing the blue shirt. "Didn't you like the brown one?" she asks. He thought he had a clear choice—the blue shirt over the brown one—but either decision he made would have been subject to challenge. This technique is well known to us. In the therapeutic context, however, it is not used to control but to effect positive change. Below is an example of the technique used therapeutically:

A client is asked this seemingly absurd question: "Do you want to gain control over your problem this week or the next? This is probably too soon. Perhaps you prefer a longer pause—maybe three or four weeks?" This statement suggests that the client has the power to postpone the implied improvement; it also implies that the client could just as well improve today. By leaving the timing to the client, the therapist implies that there is no question—or doubt—about the actual improvement. That the client will gain control over his problem is not a matter for negotiation or choice. The illusion of choice is created, however, by offering the client some freedom in deciding when this will happen. This technique is unlikely to work if the client perceives that the choice being offered is for the personal benefit of the therapist. In such cases, the client simply refuses to enter the frame and instead rejects both alternatives.

There are many applications of this technique to the pastoral context. It may be used, for example, to motivate a congregation or committee to take action on a desirable project or goal: "Do you want to schedule the meeting with the Urban Task Force two weeks from now, as they suggest, or would you rather allow yourselves a month's time to prepare for it?" Or, "Would you like to include this change in the order of worship in every service, or would you prefer to do it on alternate Sundays?" Putting the decision this way, the pastor precludes the option of refusing to meet with the task force or rejecting the order-of-worship change. As with its therapeutic uses, this strategy will work if the outcome is not perceived to be for the pastor's own benefit. Thus, it should not be used in situations where the pastor is perceived to have a strong personal investment in the result. In that case, the congregation or committee will simply refuse to enter the frame and will reject both alternatives.

PROVIDING A WORSE ALTERNATIVE

While therapists who use the reframing method are benevolently motivated, they are not unwilling to be hard on clients who are not cooperative when this behavior is in the client's interest. Sometimes this action involves offering something the person does not like so that he or she will choose something else. Sometimes a threat or procedure is used so the person will change in order to avoid something worse. The object is to ensure that keeping the problem is more difficult than giving it up. One way this is done is to provide the client with a worse alternative:

An elderly gentleman had a fear of riding in an elevator, and sought professional help. Noting that the man was very proper and prudish, married to an equally proper and prudish wife, the therapist (Milton Erickson) decided to use a strategy which exploited these traits. The elevators in Erickson's building were operated by young girls, and Erickson made special arrangements with one of them to assist him in his plan. He went with the gentleman to the girl's elevator. They entered, Erickson told her to close the door, and said, "Let's go up." She took the car up one story and stopped between floors. The gentleman started to yell, "What's wrong?" Erickson replied, "The elevator operator wants to kiss you." Shocked, the gentleman said, "But I'm a married man!" The girl replied, "I don't mind that." She walked toward him, and he stepped back and said, "You start the elevator." So she started it. She went up to about the fourth floor and stopped it again between floors. She said, "I just have a craving for a kiss." The man said, "You go about your business," and motioned to her to start the elevator moving again. But she replied, "Well, let's go down and start all over again," and began to take the elevator down. He said, "Not down, up!" He didn't want to go through the ordeal all over again. She started up and again stopped the car between floors and said, "Do you promise that you'll ride down in my elevator with me when you're through with your business?" He said, "I'll promise anything if you promise not to kiss me." He continued up, relieved and without fear—at least, of the elevator!—and could ride one from then on.[13]

The technique of avoiding a worse alternative is frequently used by pastors without their awareness. They typically use it to achieve cooperation with congregational or pastoral policies and goals. A pastor may explain to a confirmation class or a couple desiring a church wedding that he could have assigned more work, more meetings, or more counseling sessions than he did. The pastor's predecessor is sometimes invoked: "If Pastor Hansen were still here, you would have had to do twice as much memorization." By making the technique explicit, however, the pastor may reduce or limit its potential for genuine reframing. As the above example from Erickson indicates, it was important for the older gentleman to choose between the alternatives of riding the elevator or being kissed by the elevator operator. The perception of having a genuine choice, and acting on this choice, is what enables the individual to experience the avoidance of a worse alternative.

Therefore, if faced with the prospect of noncooperation, the pastor would do well to present the class or the couple with two alternatives and allow them to select the better of the two. By choosing, they are assuming ownership of the one selected and can no longer claim that their subsequent actions are merely in compliance, or noncompliance, with the pastor's orders. The pastor, for example, may inform a couple that premarital counseling can be done in either three or seven sessions, and invite them to choose the option that suits them best. While some couples may prefer the seven, most will choose three. Some pastors may regret a couple's choosing the smaller number of sessions, but a great deal has actually been achieved by their selection. They will have a much greater sense of ownership over the counseling process and their involvement in it than if they had simply been told to come for three sessions. They are more likely to be present for each of the three scheduled meetings, knowing that there might have been seven. They are also more likely to make positive use of their time, hoping to show the pastor that they can achieve in three sessions what other couples achieve in seven.

RELABELING

The technique of relabeling involves giving a different name to behavior and attitudes than the one the counselee has applied to them. The new label is an improvement over the original one because it more adequately describes the facts of the situation. The following is an example of relabeling:

Mr. and Mrs. Blackright had been coming to their pastor for marriage counseling. This particular evening, Mrs. Blackright related an incident in which Mr. Blackright spilled a pitcher of orange juice on the kitchen floor:[14]

PASTOR: What happened then?

MRS. B: I came charging in, yelled at him to be more careful, and then cleaned up the mess.

PASTOR: Why did *you* clean it up?

MRS. B: I knew he'd take hours to get around to it, and he'd make another mess in cleaning up that one!

PASTOR: (To Mr. Blackright) How did you feel about her cleaning up the mess?

MR. B: She's a perfectionist! Always after me to do something! I can never do anything well enough to please her! She wouldn't have liked the way I cleaned up the floor.

PASTOR: Anything else?

MR. B: (With a sly smile) Well, I suppose I knew that if I waited a little while she'd do it.

In this interchange, Mrs. Blackright labels her husband a *messy* person, while Mr. Blackright labels her a *perfectionist.* But this particular episode does not substantiate such labels. A person who spills a pitcher of orange juice may be viewed as *messy,* but we normally think of a messy person as one who leaves dirty clothes on the floor, allows dishes to accumulate in the sink, and lets his or her desk become cluttered with miscellaneous papers, junk mail, and half-eaten Twinkies. A person who spills a pitcher of orange juice is not necessarily messy. He or she may be described as *clumsy* or *accident prone.* Furthermore, a person who feels that spilled orange juice should be cleaned up as soon as possible is not necessarily a *perfectionist.* A perfectionist is someone who has an inordinate or excessive need to have things just right or just so. The need to clean up spills could as well be characteristic of *cleanliness, orderliness,* or even *safety consciousness.*

Because the labels of *messy* and *perfectionist* are not self-evidently accurate, the counselor is prompted to look for more adequate words to describe the reported behavior or attitudes. On the basis of this episode, a more accurate label for Mr. Blackright would be *dependent,* since he acts toward his wife like a little boy who relies on his mother to set things right, and complains that she expects too much from him. And Mrs. Blackright may be described as a person who *dominates* her husband, insisting on doing things for him which he could easily do for himself. These labels have the advantage of describing the relationship between the two clients, whereas the ones they had used attributed fixed personality traits to each other. The new labels imply that change is possible since altering the way they relate to one another is much more feasible for them than changing fixed personality traits. And judging from their own self-descriptions, especially Mrs. Blackright's portrayal of herself as "charging in" and "yelling at him," it seems quite apparent that they would like to change the way they relate to one another.

The technique of relabeling is especially useful in pastoral ministry when the original labels support inertia, or resistance to change, and the new label offered by the pastor invites the belief that change is really possible. When pastors relabel the behavior of individuals, of groups, or of the congregation as a whole, they should choose words to describe the present situation as the effect of mutable rather than immutable factors so as to reinforce the conviction that desirable change is quite possible. For example, it is much better to say that one's church is *a sleeping giant* than to say that it is *dead.* While Christians believe that the dead can come back to life, we all agree that it is easier for the sleeping to be awakened, as sleeping does not imply a fixed state. Labels describing ways of relating rather than traits are especially helpful in showing that change, in a very fundamental and dramatic way, is a real possibility.

PREEMPTING

In preempting, the therapist anticipates the client's resistance and preempts it. The therapist may say, "There is a relatively simple solution for this problem, but knowing that your work involves complex ideas, I am almost sure that you will not like it." Or, "I know that few people would look at your situation in this way, but . . ." Such preemptings almost demand agreement with the therapist's next point because they imply that disagreement would be a sign of limited understanding, lack of imagination, or courage. A close derivative of preempting is formulations through which one says something by claiming that one does not or would not say it: "If I were not your therapist, I would simply point out that . . ." Or,

"If your wife were not here, I would say that . . ." Or, "To somebody less desperate and troubled than you I would probably say quite frankly that I consider this problem rather trivial."[15]

Following is an example of the therapeutic use of the technique of preempting:

A therapist was working with a client who had gone through a number of relationships in which she had successfully maneuvered a man to make a commitment to her, only to inform him that he was moving too fast, whereupon he would terminate the relationship. Now she was becoming involved with another man. The therapist could see that the pattern was beginning to repeat itself, but was also certain that the woman would not accept this observation, that she would accuse the therapist of trying to discourage her efforts to find a man or of being jealous. So he made the following preemptive statement: "I was going to say something about your new relationship, but caught myself, since I realized that you had surely thought of it yourself, it is so patently obvious." The client asked, "Well, what was it? What were you about to say?" Then the therapist put forward his theory, and she, having already been told that he believed she would easily have thought of it herself, agreed that it had indeed occurred to her as well, and that the idea had some merit. In this way, she was more receptive to his theory than she would have been if he had simply put it forward without the preemptive comment.

In the pastoral setting, this technique is especially useful for situations in which the pastor suspects that she will not gain a hearing. She might, for example, note her very superficial understanding of the business matter which is before the church council because her theological education was anything but practical. This comment preempts the tendency of some council members to dismiss the pastor's views on business matters on the grounds that pastors (especially women pastors) lack good business sense. This preemptive strike does not guarantee that her suggestion will be adopted, but does increase the likelihood that it will gain a fair and sympathetic hearing.

PRESCRIPTION

The prescription technique involves giving a client a prescription, much as a medical doctor prescribes certain medicines. The prescription may have a direct connection with the client's problems (that is, have its basis in the therapist's actual diagnosis of the problem), but this is not an absolute requirement. The prescription may be more like a placebo, effective merely because the client has confidence in it. Below is an example of how the prescription technique works:

A student once approached Milton Erickson with concern about a maiden aunt who had made multiple suicide attempts. Instead of attempting to arrange an appointment at his office, Erickson appeared the next day at the woman's home where she lived alone with her maid. When she came to the door, he introduced himself and asked to be given a tour of the house. Surprised but intrigued, she agreed to show him her home. In the sun porch, he noticed a row of pots containing African violets. She told him that she had a talent for growing these plants. He also learned that she went to church every Sunday, but otherwise had no meaningful social life. Upon leaving, he said to her, "Madam, here is your prescription. I want you to send your maid to the nursery to purchase many more pots and every available strain of African violet. Furthermore, whenever a child is born to a member of your congregation, I want you to give a pot of African violets to the parents at the baptism. Whenever a wedding is celebrated, I want you to give a pot of these flowers to the bride." Twenty years later, he clipped an article from the local newspaper, "The African Violet Queen Dies at Age 76 . . ." it began, and recounted a touching tale of how appreciated this woman had been in her church and community. In telling this story to a group of therapists shortly before his death, Erickson concluded with the remark, "I never did know what was wrong with that woman."[16] The issue here is not whether Erickson knew the causes of the woman's problems, but that she had faith in his prescription. Her faith, however, was not blind, since his prescription undoubtedly made good sense to her.

One of the most common pastoral uses of the prescription technique is to employ the Bible prescriptively, as when selected biblical verses are applied to counselees' problems. Frequently, however, these prescriptions fail to embrace all the known facts and are therefore unsuccessful in reframing the problem. Prescriptions based on the type of pastoral wisdom reflected in Erickson's intervention with the suicidal woman are more effective because they take the individual herself into account. Yet, because the more liberal pastors have shunned the prescriptive use of the Bible, they have not made much use of the prescription technique.[17] Furthermore, prescription is generally more acceptable among parishioners who hold pastors in high authority, and this, too, is less likely to be the case in the more liberal traditions. Yet, from another view, the prescription technique may work among liberal church members precisely because it is unexpected and not something to which they are accustomed. A minister may prescribe to a depressed parishioner that each morning she sing "Jesus Loves Me." Even if she does not actually follow the prescription, the idea that the pastor would make such a proposal may be sufficiently unusual or amusing to effect an attitude change. And certainly, this approach is better than more direct efforts to cheer her up, for, as we saw in chapter 1, such efforts usually make matters worse.

Some years ago, when I was experiencing what I would call "despair," I found myself returning again and again to Psalm 131. Its brevity was such that I was able to memorize it:

> O Lord, my heart is not lifted up,
>> my eyes are not raised too high,
> I do not occupy myself with things
>> too great and too marvelous for me.
> But I have calmed and quieted my soul, . . .
>> like a child that is quieted is my soul.

This psalm was a prescription for me, a powerful set of words that gave me the assurance I would somehow get through that difficult time.

THE SURRENDER TACTIC

In *The Power Tactics of Jesus,* Jay Haley notes that many animals assume a helpless posture before a stronger adversary. This tactic incapacitates the opponent, making him unable to attack and kill the weaker animal. Haley contends that this is the strategy behind Jesus' instruction to his followers to respond to the one who smites them on the one cheek by offering the other cheek as well. The tactic "has been proved effective by weeping wives and by anxious parents who find that helplessness will enforce their directives more tyrannically than giving orders. The extreme tactic of threat of suicide falls into a similar category." This technique may also be used therapeutically, especially in situations where the client is very strong-willed and aggressive.[18] The following is an example of its therapeutic use:

A client was certain that he was better than the therapist at diagnosing his problem. Whenever the therapist would offer an interpretation, the client would reject it in favor of one which he considered more accurate or insightful. The result was a power struggle between therapist and client, and no significant change in the client. Finally, the therapist decided that the conflict was fruitless and he employed the surrender tactic. He acknowledged to the client that he was no match for the client's superior therapeutic insight, and that he had come to the conclusion that there are certain clients whom he will never be able to help because they are actually better therapists than he is. This statement utterly disarmed the client, and he became far more cooperative and considerably less resistant in subsequent therapy sessions.

Many congregations have members who believe they know more than the pastor about how to pastor. This often precipitates a power struggle between the pastor and these parishioners. By employing the surrender tactic, the pastor is not only able to break the pattern of escalating conflict, but is also able to exercise much greater control over what is to happen between the two of them. As Haley puts it, "You cannot defeat a helpless opponent"; thus, the surrender tactic is not a sign of weakness, but of strength. Pastors who are weak, or perceive themselves to be weak, will often struggle to gain power over difficult parishioners, only to find they are defeated anyway. It is better in such situations to yield, for surrender deprives one's adversary of the ultimate victory he desires. However, it should be noted that the surrender tactic is usually used by therapists only *in extremis,* as a last resort, after other techniques have failed.[19] A pastor who uses the surrender tactic as a first or second resort will be perceived as cowardly and unable to stand up for himself. This technique works only when there has been a fairly longstanding power struggle, and continuing it is fruitless.

CONCLUSION

We have reviewed a number of techniques that are used by therapists to effect a reframing of a situation. I do not expect that all of these will appeal to every reader of this book. But I am certain that every reader will find something of value in them. I also realize that some readers will perceive these methods to be inappropriate for pastors, as they often involve a certain amount of playfulness, fictionalizing, and pretending—though I would emphasize that lying or misrepresenting the pastor's views is never appropriate in the use of reframing. Still, some readers may feel that even fictionalizing and pretending is unbecoming in a pastor, that it compromises the pastor's integrity. I believe, however, that the motivation to help people change, and for the better, is the important consideration, and that a certain amount of playfulness and pretending is not inappropriate if it will help a person envision and realize a more abundant, less painful life. After all, the pastor is not using these techniques against the person, but against the dysfunctional attitudes, behaviors, and beliefs which the person, implicitly at least, wants changed. Reframing techniques are designed to out-maneuver the dysfunctions which are causing pain and discomfort, allowing the creative energies of the client to emerge instead. The techniques work precisely because the therapist respects the clients and regards each one as a unique and special individual. Jesus out-maneuvered the demons precisely because he had deep respect for the persons who were in their control. Without such respect, "reframing will be a hollow and transparent lie designed to manipulate the client for the therapist's own benefit."[20]

Also, the role played by pretense in reframing ought not to be exaggerated; in many cases, no pretense is necessary. For the most part, reframing relies on playfulness, which effects change through humor and a lighthearted, infectious optimism. Surely there can be nothing inherently wrong with pastors being playful, even in situations where persons are experiencing pain. Indeed, painful situations are precisely the place where it may be terribly wrong for the pastor to engage in anything less—or more—than playful reframing.

So reframing techniques are not weapons to be used in a manipulative or controlling manner. They are methods that break impasses, making positive change possible. Good reframers are not "con-artists" who view other people as potential victims; they are "pro-artists" whose creative imagination is for the sole purpose of enabling others to have fuller, more abundant lives. The real manipulators, the real con-artists, are those who control others through subtle, or not-so-subtle, techniques of double-binding. In contrast, good reframers are concerned to help untie the knots, so that victims of such manipulation may experience, at last, the freedom that God had forever intended them to have.

PART 2

The Pastoral Care of Reframing

CHAPTER THREE
Reframing—
The Ministry
of Jesus

Difficulties are a fact of human existence. Problems are extended difficulties, maintained by mishandling. Such mishandling can take one of three forms: first, simplification in which the needed action is not taken, either because the difficulty is denied or because it is minimized; second, utopianism in which the action undertaken is misdirected toward an unattainable goal; or third, efforts toward first-order, more-of-the-same change, where second-order change is required.

Often, the ministry of Jesus is misused in pastoral care to simplify, to misdirect, or to effect the wrong-order change. Our bad experiences with efforts to apply Jesus' ministry to contemporary situations makes one cautious about proposing still another such application. Yet, I would argue that Jesus' ministry focused on second-order change, especially in situations where first-order change techniques had already been applied, but to no avail. For example, Luke (4:16-30) tells us that it was Jesus' custom to worship in a synagogue and to read the Scriptures in public. Near the beginning of his ministry, Jesus was given the scroll of Isaiah from which he read:

> The spirit of the Lord is upon me,
>   because he has anointed me to preach good news to the poor.
> He has sent me to proclaim release to the captives
>   and recovering of sight to the blind,
> to set at liberty those who are oppressed,
>   to proclaim the acceptable year of the Lord.

When Jesus sat down and, with all eyes focused on him, said, "Today this Scripture has been fulfilled in your hearing," he reframed the worship of Nazareth, creating for it an ethos of second-order change. Everyone spoke well of him as they wondered, "Is not this Joseph's son?" When Jesus told them that a prophet is not welcome in his own country and that the earlier prophets healed not Jews but foreigners, the people rose up to put him out of the city. Yet he walked through their midst, unhurt.

This reframing set the stage for Jesus' ministry as a whole, as it created expectations that he would not be content with anything less than second-order change. In this sense, I find reframing to be characteristic not only of his own ministry but also of the ministries of those who have faithfully followed in his footsteps. Indeed, one of the most noted features of his ministry—both in its intention and in its effect—is that it all fit together, and somehow, what held it together was his commitment to second-order change. His teaching ministry—through parables, proverbs, and prophetic utterances—was fully consistent with his healing ministry. These were two sides of the same coin. Jesus sought significant change in the minds, hearts, and bodies of individuals by enabling them to think about things differently, to see the world in a new way, and to experience a new openness. My purpose in this chapter is to identify the second-order changing, the reframing nature of Jesus' teaching and healing ministry. In the following two chapters, I will apply reframing methods in Jesus' ministry of teaching (chapter 4) and healing (chapter 5) to contemporary pastoral care situations, contrasting the effectiveness of his reframing techniques with the inadequate results of the mishandling of difficulties.

REFRAMING IN JESUS' PARABLES

The teaching ministry of Jesus contains several different types of discourse: sayings, proverbs, instructions, and parables. While each exhibits the character of reframing, the parables are especially informative for ministry in which significant change is desired. Nevertheless, following are brief examples of reframing through these other types of discourse.

In Matthew's Gospel, Jesus is depicted as teaching in the synagogues, preaching the gospel of the kingdom, and healing every disease (Matt. 4:23). The first sample of his teaching is given in "The Sermon on the Mount." The Beatitudes are excellent examples of reframing; they declare that, even now, a person's situation may be dramatically different from how it appears: "Blessed are the poor in spirit, for theirs is the kingdom of heaven" (Matt. 5:3). A little later Jesus illustrates his understanding of the law through a series of proverbs: "You have heard that it was said to the men of old, 'You shall not kill; and whoever kills shall be liable to judgment.' But I say to you that every one who is angry with his brother shall be liable to judgment." (Matt. 5:21-22). This, of course, is a reframing. Even in his direct teaching, as when he tells his followers not to heap up empty phrases but to pray "like this" (Matt. 6:7-13), Jesus is engaging in reframing.

It is the parables, however, on which I want to focus here. There are at least three different ways that Jesus utilizes parables for reframing. At the end of some, he declares the new frame through which the parable is to be viewed. In the midst of others, he has one of the characters enact a new frame. In a third group, a reframing is neither enacted by one of the characters nor declared by Jesus, the storyteller. Yet, even in this group, Jesus is able to reframe the situation in which he finds himself.

The Reframe Is Declared by the Storyteller

In many of his parables, Jesus relates a human interaction and then proposes the frame through which this action is newly to be understood. Take, for example, the parable Jesus told about the man who had two sons (Matt. 21:28-31). The man went to the first and said, "Son, go and work in the vineyard today." And he answered, "I will not." But afterward he repented and went. Then the man went to the second son and said the same thing. This son answered, "I go, sir," but did not go. Jesus then turns to his audience and asks, "Which of the two did the will of his father?"

"Will of his father" is the frame in which the story is to be understood. This frame defines and explains the interactions between father and sons. Another frame would give these interactions a totally different meaning. If Jesus had turned to his audience and asked what the story tells us about the younger generation, these interactions would have been understood very differently. Instead of responding, "The first son," someone in the audience might have blurted out, "The younger generation is no damn good. They either sass you or they lie to you." In this frame, both sons are condemned. Instead, the frame Jesus used—"will of his father"—forced listeners to choose between the two sons: this one did his father's will, this one did not. "Will of his father" and "younger generation" are two different frames yielding two very different conclusions. The frame that Jesus uses, however, forces the hearers to rethink the whole issue of faithfulness: it is not a matter of words but of actions.

Another example is the parable Jesus told to some who trusted in themselves and their own righteousness (Luke 18:9-14). Jesus describes two men going up to pray in the temple. The first, a representative self-righteous person, offers an eloquent prayer. He thanks God that he is not like others who have gone astray. He concludes by listing signs of his devotion: he fasts twice a week and he tithes on everything. In contrast is the tax collector who has also entered the temple to pray. He neither approaches God with confidence nor proclaims any signs of his devotion. He looks down into his sinfulness and calls upon God's mercy. Then Jesus declares the frame in which this episode is to be understood: "I tell you, this man went down to his house *justified* rather than the other; for everyone who exalts himself will be humbled, but he who humbles himself will be exalted."

The original frame of Jesus' hearers was apparently "righteous before others." From that frame, the first man in the parable had ample reason to be righteous—he was not like others. But Jesus introduces the new frame of being "justified before God." It was the second man, and not the first, the hearers are told, who went home at one with God. Why? Because God is reframing the world, humbling those who exalt themselves and exalting those who humble themselves. The new frame points to a God who is actively shaking the foundations, challenging the status quo.

Jesus could even use the situations others presented to him in a parabolic manner, giving them a new, unaccustomed frame. For example, when told that his mother and brothers had come asking for him, he replies, "Who is my mother, and who are my brothers?" Then, stretching out his hand toward his disciples, he says, "Here are my mothers and my brothers!" (Matt. 12:49). At another time a man runs up to him and asks, "Good teacher, what must I do to inherit eternal life?" Jesus does not answer the question but challenges the mode of address: "Why do you call me good? No one is good but God alone" (Mark 10:18). So, in these two stories, he reframes the situation by challenging the others' assumptions about the interaction taking place. In the first case, he questions the identity of those who sought him. In the second, he questions the identity that was assigned to him.

In both his parables and parabolic utterances, Jesus' teaching ministry was characterized by reframings which he offered his hearers, challenging them to see the situation in a very different light, within a frame of reference to which they were unaccustomed.

Reframing Effected by a Character

Even more characteristic of Jesus' teaching ministry is his use of a character within the parable who enacts a new frame. An example is the story of the judge (Luke 18:1-8) who neither feared God nor cared about people, and the widow who kept coming to him and saying, "Vindicate me against my adversary." For a while, the judge refused, but, after a time, he said to himself, "Though I neither fear God nor regard man, yet because this widow bothers me, I will vindicate her, or she will wear me out by her continual coming."

Here, a character in the story, the judge, sets the frame for understanding the meaning of the action. His behavior cannot be attributed to his sense of righteousness or concern for justice, but to the fact that he finds the widow bothersome. The frame is not "justice" but "self-interest," which defines the meaning of his actions. The message of the parable is that one is more likely to get a fair hearing by being a nuisance than by appealing to the other's sense of justice. In Luke's account, however, the story undergoes another reframing, as the action of the judge is compared to God's vindication of his elect: "And the Lord said, 'Hear what the unrighteous judge says. And will not God vindicate his elect, who cry to him day and night? Will he delay long over them? I tell you, he will vindicate them speedily.' " This seems to alter the original frame of the story from motives for vindicating someone to the vindication itself, suggesting that those who call upon God for deliverance will surely be heard. Perhaps it reduces the radicalness of the originally told story which advised appealing to others' self-interest for vindication. In Luke's frame, self-interested motivation is dropped, for God, after all, does not act from self-interest.

The parable of the wheat and tares (Matt. 13:24-30) provides another instance in which a character reframes the situation. A man's enemy sowed weeds among the wheat that the man had planted. When the plants came up and bore grain, the weeds also appeared. The man's servants reported what was happening, and proposed to go out and gather up the weeds. But he said, "No, lest in gathering the weeds you root up the wheat along with them. Let both grow together until the harvest; and at harvest time I will tell the reapers, 'Gather the weeds first and bind them in bundles to be burned, but gather the wheat into my barn.'" His enemy's plan to subvert him was thereby foiled. What made the crucial difference was his rejection of his servants' solution to the problem, a solution based on the common-sense idea that the offensive weeds needed to be removed. Instead, he saw that no real harm would be done by allowing the wheat and the weeds to mature together, and separating them later. This was a reframing of the problem which led to a second-order change. His enemy's plan to destroy his crop had failed.

Another example is the parable of the laborers in the vineyard (Matt. 20:1-16). When the workers complained of unfairness, the vineyard owner reframed the situation from "fairness" to "generosity." To a worker who complained that those who worked only one hour were paid the same as those who had worked the whole day, the owner said, "Friend, I am doing you no wrong; did you not agree with me for a denarius? Take what belongs to you and go; I choose to give this last as I give to you. Am I not allowed to do what I choose with what belongs to me? Or do you begrudge my generosity?" By thus reframing the situation, the owner did not address the worker's legitimate questions of fairness, but instead gave the situation a new framework and challenged the worker to view it from this radically new perspective: not "what's fair" but "what's generous."

In these three examples, the hearer of the parable is given a different perspective from which to view the world as a character in the story enacts a new frame. To be sure, in these examples and others, Jesus (or the Gospel writer) goes on to extend that meaning for the hearer (or reader). But the implication for the hearer of the story is a radical change or reframing of reality.

The Reframing Does Not Seem to Work

The third group of parables are those that do not seem to work as reframings. Indeed, like Jesus' announcement at Nazareth—"Today, the Scripture has been fulfilled in your hearing" (Luke 4:21)—the result seems to be anger and confusion, not new and liberating insight. Instead of producing followers, the parables seem to produce antagonists. Yet, even here, I would say that a reframing is nonetheless occurring.

One of the parables is the story of the wicked tenants (Matt. 21:33-41). The vineyard owner sent a group of servants to collect his fruits from the tenants. When they arrived, the tenants set upon and killed them. When he sent another group of servants, "more than the first," these too were set upon and killed. In an attempt to reframe the situation, the owner decided to send his son to the tenants, saying, "They will respect my son." But when they saw his son, they said to one another, "This is the heir; come let us kill him and have his inheritance." Evidently, they assumed the son had come to them because his father had died or was seriously ill. By killing the son, they expected to get their hands on everything that belonged to the owner.

Thus, the owner's attempt to reframe the situation by sending his son instead of another group of servants was unsuccessful. The reason it failed is that it took insufficient account of the evidence presented by his first two efforts: the tenants were vicious men who would stop at nothing in their intent to defraud the owner of what was rightfully his. If they had killed two groups of servants, why assume they would not kill again? A more adequate reframing would be based on the judgment that they would kill again if they had opportunity to do so. The son's appearance played right into their hands. His appearance resulted in "more of the same."

But this is not the end of the story. The owner has now had enough of the wicked tenants. He kills them, and gives the vineyard to other tenants. This action was a successful reframing of the situation, and possibly the only reframing left to the owner. Certainly, he had sufficient provocation for this response. After the tenants had killed his son, how could he possibly contemplate any less severe action against them? However, if we consider the eventual fate of the storyteller (i.e., death by crucifixion), as Matthew surely does, we sense that the parable itself seems to have failed. In this case, the owner (God) had ample evidence that he was dealing with people who were unlikely to show "respect" for anyone, including his own son (Jesus). Yet, God failed to take such evidence into account, and exposed his son to a situation which could lead only to death by violence. Thus, the only way the parable works is in the light of the resurrection stories, the most dramatic reframings of all. The death of Jesus is now understood to be part of a divine strategy of paradoxical intention, in which the death of God's son makes victory over death possible for all those who believe in him.

A parable in which no reframing seems to be attempted is the story of the hidden talent (Matt. 25:14-30). Its focal figure is the third servant who hid his talent because his master was a hard man, reaping where he did not sow, and gathering where he did not winnow. When his master returned, however, the servant was severely chastised because he had acted out of fear. The master acknowledged that the servant was right to fear him, but pointed out that the servant could have acted differently on the basis of his fear. For instance, he could have invested the money with the bankers so that his master would at least have gotten the talent plus interest. This is a case, then, where no effort was made to reframe the situation, where the servant assumed that he had no alternative but to hide the talent. However, the master pointed out that an alternative *was* possible. Reframing "reveals that what appeared unchangeable can indeed be changed and that there exist superordinate alternatives."[1] Thus, even if one must deal with a master who is a "very hard man," there may be alternative courses of action. Even if the servant acted out of fear, there are better alternatives than the course he chose.

Jesus closes this parable (in Matthew's account) with a reframing of his own: If anyone chooses to respond to the situation with a closed—an anti-reframing—mind, this person will lose everything that he has and be cast into outer darkness. In contrast, those who respond in a creative, resourceful way will receive even more. Thus, the parable is a lesson to those who refuse to reframe their situation, but instead, out of fear, cling to the status quo.

Even in the parables in which the reframing does not seem to work internally, Jesus (according to the Gospel writers) still seems to be reframing the world of his hearers. The owner who sent his son to collect from the tenants did not acknowledge their wickedness until his son had been killed. The servant who was fearful of the master hid the talent and realized his error only when the master had returned and demanded an accounting. The failure of these characters to reframe the situation is the lesson of the parables, allowing Jesus to make the point that reframing can be a matter of life and death. Reframing leads to life, abundant life, while failure to reframe leads to death, to weeping and gnashing of teeth.

REFRAMING THROUGH ACTS OF HEALING

I would not want to claim that all of Jesus' acts of healing are examples of reframing. When Jesus came to the house of Jairus and declared that his daughter was not dead but only sleeping (Mark 5:21-24, 35-43), this action was, on one level, a reframing (i.e., a situation defined by others as "death" is reframed by Jesus as "sleeping"). But certainly there is more to the story than this reframing, for the young girl was, in fact, dead. We are told that the change occurred not when Jesus declared her to be asleep but when she responded to his command: "Little girl, I say to you, arise." Surely, then, Jesus' power over the forces of death involved an authority greater than his ability to reframe. Still, like his parables, his healings frequently employed reframing strategies and techniques.

I would draw attention to three types of healings in which reframing actions were present. In some of the healings, Jesus prescribes an action. In other healings, he attributes them not to his own power or ability, but to the faith of the person healed. In a third group, he treats the supplicant in a paradoxical fashion.

Healing Through a Prescribed Action

As one might expect, Jesus acted in an authoritative manner in some healings. Several healings occur when he prescribes some action to be performed. In these, the prescription removes an internal fear or blockage from the person.

The man who had been lying near the pool at Bethzatha for some years is an excellent case in point (John 5:2-18). He had been relying on a quite fruitless plan for healing: when the water began to bubble, he would look around for someone to help him into the pool. Finding no one, he would try to maneuver himself into the water, but someone would always get there before him. Even though the plan had not been working, the man had been lying there for thirty-eight years. Jesus asked him if he wanted to be healed, then *prescribed* a much simpler approach: "Rise, take up your pallet, and walk." At once the man was cured, and he got up. Aside from infusing him with strength, Jesus was encouraging the man to look at his situation from a new perspective. If he could move himself laterally toward the pool, why could he not assume a horizontal position? It was as though this solution was too simple, too obvious, and so the man had clung for thirty-eight years to a more elaborate plan. We can also notice how Jesus was reframing the world of others on that day for it was the Sabbath when Jesus told the man to take up his pallet. This violation of the law angered many; when Jesus announced that "my Father is working still, and I am working" (i.e., not resting on the Sabbath), the listeners were infuriated and sought to kill him.

A similar issue of work on the Sabbath surrounds another healing: that of the man of withered hand (Mark 3:1-6). In the synagogue Jesus calls the man to himself and poses the question, "Is it lawful on the sabbath to do good or to do harm, to save life or to kill?" We are told that Jesus looked around in anger at those who sought to accuse him and he grieved at their hardness of heart. Then he told the man to stretch out his hand and the hand was restored. Apart from the question of how the hand was actually healed, we can see that Jesus was reframing the situation itself, refusing to debate first-order change issues when second-order change was needed and possible.

Another healing which involved a prescribed action occurred when Jesus instructed the ten lepers to go and show themselves to the priests, and they were healed en route (Luke 17:11-19). This healing may be viewed as a prescription based on the concept that it is usually better to advertise than to conceal one's infirmities. By instructing the lepers to go and show themselves, Jesus was encouraging them to display, not to conceal, their condition. By agreeing to display themselves, they were healed. The healing, in turn, led to a further reframing as one of the lepers returned to thank Jesus, and it happened that he was a Samaritan. Jesus expressed dismay that only this foreigner had returned, and, in a reframing that must have galled many of his listeners, he assured the Samaritan that it was his faith that had made him well.

In these and other such healings, Jesus was reframing the situations of those who had languished under an internal fear or blockage. The suggestion is not necessarily that those who are similarly afflicted today (e.g., are phobic) can be as suddenly rid of their disability. It does imply, however, that many suffer in diminished worlds of their own making, trapped by their own fruitless plans and useless routines, and that a prescription which cuts to the heart of the fear or inhibition can effect a dramatic change.

Healings Attributed to Faith

On many occasions Jesus minimized his own curative powers and instead attributed healings to the faith of the person healed. In these instances, he reframed the usual physician-patient relationship, refusing to be viewed as the omnipotent physician.

The story of the woman with an issue of blood (Mark 5:25-34) is one example of this. She "had suffered much under many physicians, and had spent all that she had, and was no better but rather grew worse." These efforts had resulted in "more of the same." But when she touched Jesus' garment, he perceived "in himself that power had gone forth from him," as though the healing was an involuntary act. Unlike the physicians who had made conscious efforts to heal her, and had charged her for them, Jesus had not even tried to help her. Indeed, he was upset with her for taking advantage of his power without his knowledge or prior approval. When she confessed to what she had done, he did not claim to have healed her, but attributed what happened between them to her own faith. What others would view as an act of desperation, he saw as an act of faith. All this was a reframing.

Another instance occurs when the centurion approaches Jesus for the sake of a paralyzed and distressed servant (Matt. 8:5-13). Jesus says that he will come and heal the servant. But the centurion answers, "Lord, I am not worthy of having you in my house; but only say the word and my servant will be healed." The non-Jewish military officer understands that, just as he can command soldiers, so Jesus can command this situation. Jesus is struck by the faith this Gentile displays, and says that many like him will sit at the table of Abraham, Isaac, and Jacob, while the presumed heirs will be cast out. Then Jesus tells the man to go, for the servant will be healed as the officer believed he would be. Again, the relation of physician-patient, analogous to that of officer-soldier, is reframed by Jesus: the healing has occurred because the other had faith. Neither person—the woman with the issue of blood or the centurion—was drawn into a dependency relationship with Jesus as a result of the healing. On the contrary, both were free to go their own way, for their faith had effected the healing.

Healings That Employ Paradoxical Intentionality

In the first type of healing, Jesus prescribes an action that alters the situation. In the second type, he attributes the result to the faith of the person. In this type, Jesus sets the stage for healing by treating the supplicant in a paradoxical fashion.

A Syrophoenician woman came to Jesus and begged him to cast the demon out of her daughter (Mark 7:24-30). But Jesus replied, "Let the children first be fed, for it is not right to take the children's bread and throw it to the dogs." To this, she answered, "Yes, Lord; yet even the dogs under the table eat the children's crumbs." This was a shrewd response, as it asserted that it is not true that the dogs can be fed only at the children's expense, and Jesus responded in kind: "For this saying you may go your way; the demon has left your daughter." Here, Jesus advances a plausible reason for why he ought not help her, and she successfully counters this reasoning in her reply. Because Jesus agrees with her—one doesn't gain only at the expense of the other—he responds to her plea for help.

In the story of the Gerasene demoniac (Mark 5:1-20), Jesus, paradoxically, cures the man by allowing the demons to try to prove Jesus wrong. As Jesus approached, he said to the demons, "Come out of the man, you unclean spirit!" In response, the demon-possessed man cried out, "What have you to do with me, Jesus?"

Then Jesus asked, "What is your name?" He replied, "My name is Legion, for we are many." Then the man begged Jesus not to send the demons out of the country. The demons instead begged him to allow them to enter a great herd of swine feeding nearby on the hillside. Jesus agreed; the demons left the man, entering the swine, and the maddened swine rushed down the steep bank into the sea where they drowned. In effect, the demons' denial of Jesus' right to have anything to do with them ("What do you have to do with us?") play directly into Jesus' hands. They propose their own resolution so as not to be sent out from the region, and the possession ends as the swine rush into the sea and are drowned. This attempt by the demons to prove that Jesus has no control over them is, in fact, the reframing and the healing. Thus, the paradox here is that Jesus does not prescribe the healing, but allows the demons to do it for him. The causes of the illness are thus the source of the cure. This paradoxical outcome illustrates Watzlawick's point that, often, an individual's attempt to prove a reframing false makes it necessary "to engage in the very goal which is the goal of therapy."[2] Once the demons deny Jesus' right to have anything to do with them, they have lost the day, for this very denial plays right into Jesus' hands.

Many other healing stories could be cited to support the claim that Jesus uses reframing strategies and techniques in his healing ministry. It could also be shown that he uses a variety of such strategies. We have noted that he makes particular use of prescription and paradoxical intention, two very important reframing techniques. It may also be observed that, in attributing healings to the faith of the recipient, he uses the Belloc Ploy; in responding to the demons, he employs the technique of benevolent sabotage. However, in noting that Jesus used reframing techniques employed by psychotherapists today, I am not implying that his healings were only psychological, or that their effect was attributable solely to his use of reframing methods. For the Gospel writers, the significance of his healings was certainly not that he used reframing methods, but that his healings attested to the presence of the kingdom of God in this time and place. The purpose of the healings was not to draw attention to the healer's techniques but to the power of God in their very midst. And yet, it is certainly striking that his healings involved the use of reframing for the purpose of effecting second-order changes reflective of the kingdom, the power, and the glory of God. The element shared by reframing and the kingdom of God is the commitment to second-order change.

While Jesus' teaching and healing ministries were unique in many ways, they are not without their modern-day parallels. Since the following two chapters will focus upon pastoral care cases, I would like to turn to the world of psychotherapy in order to highlight the similarities between Jesus' use of reframing and our own, in spite of the radical shifts in time and place. While there is no strict correlation between the ordering of these illustrations and the framework which I have already provided in Jesus' teaching and healing, there are, nevertheless, some connections.

MODERN CONNECTIONS

An Effective Prescription

Just as Jesus set a new frame in some parables and prescribed actions in some healings, this first case follows from a simple identification of the existing and the desired frame, and a resulting prescription.[3]

A couple had been operating a restaurant business together for many years and had quarreled constantly about its management. The wife insisted that her husband should manage it, and he protested that she never let him do so. As he put it, "Yes, she keeps telling me I should run the restaurant. All the time she's running it she tells me I should do it. I'm the bus boy, I'm the janitor, I scrub the floors. She nags at me about the buying, she nags at me about the bookkeeping, she nags at me because the floor needs scrubbing."

The therapist Milton Erickson made a detailed exploration of the elements of the situation, and learned that the couple opened their restaurant every morning at seven and closed it at ten in the evening. She had the keys, and unlocked the door in the morning and locked it again at night, while he parked or fetched the car. The frame was one in which she controlled the opening and closing of the restaurant, while the desired frame was one in which he would have greater control over the process. So Erickson gave them this apparently very simple prescription: the husband was to go to the restaurant half an hour before his wife did. They agreed to this. After all, it was simple enough.

The next day, when the husband arrived a half hour before his wife, he carried the keys. He opened the door, and he set up the restaurant for the day. When she arrived, she was completely out of step. Many things had been set in motion by him, and he was managing them. Of course, when she remained behind at home that half hour in the morning, it left her with the breakfast dishes and the housework to do before she left. She found that these activities could easily consume a half hour; as time went on, she began taking forty minutes, even an hour, to straighten up the house before going to the restaurant. In this way, she discovered that her husband could get along at the restaurant without her. Her husband, in turn, was discovering that he could indeed manage the restaurant. And once she found that the operation of the restaurant did not suffer if she arrived late in the morning, she began to leave early in the evening as well.

Thus, by bringing about this minimal change in the couple's behavior—so minimal that they did not offer any significant resistance—the therapist achieved a decisive change in their lives. This is an example of the same sort of ministry Jesus conducted, as he discerned a new way of framing the life situation, and enabled people to enter into this new frame by prescribing some new, seemingly insignificant behavior (e.g., "Pick up your pallet, and do it on a day when *others* are at rest.").

A Matter of Faith

Just as Jesus had characters enact the new frame in some of his parables, and attributed the transformation in certain healings to the faith of the individual, so in this second case a participant in the therapeutic process establishes the new frame, to which those in need of transformation voluntarily respond.

Many years ago, when I was a seminarian involved in the summer clinical pastoral education program at St. Elizabeths Hospital in Washington, D.C., I was assigned to a ward of long-term patients, many of whom had been at St. Elizabeths for twenty or thirty years. A young psychiatrist had just been assigned to the ward, and one of the changes he made was to install a small mirror on a post in the center of the ward. Previously, there had been no mirrors or glass of any kind, for fear that a patient might cut himself. In this context, installing a mirror was itself to engage in paradoxical intention: glass, previously viewed as harmful, was now being viewed as potentially therapeutic. The new mirror had a very different effect from what had been feared. At first, the men would approach the mirror hesitantly and cautiously, almost shyly, and steal a quick glance at themselves. Seeing themselves for the first time in twenty or thirty years, they were horrified at what they saw. They could scarcely believe they looked so haggard and scruffy. But this shock of recognition prompted them to begin asking for combs and razors, which were supplied to them. By the end of the summer, the men's appearance was dramatically changed, and they were also more alert and active.

The mirror—this small change in the system—had effected a dramatic transformation in the ward. The psychiatrist (a character in the story) created a new frame through his simple action of placing the mirror on the post. This action implied that the men could be trusted not to hurt themselves, and the men, thus encouraged, made a faith response. The psychiatrist could not, and did not, take credit for the change in these men. Instead, he could agree with Jesus that it was their faith that made them better. He had introduced the catalyst for change—the mirror—but it was their response, in trust and freedom, that enabled them to change.

Confronting the Demon

Finally, just as Jesus evoked reframings through parables which failed to exhibit reframings, and just as he healed through paradoxical interventions, in this case, the therapist achieves a change by taking advantage of the person's resistance to reframing, or to second-order change, causing him to play unwittingly into the therapist's hands.[4]

This is the case of Joe, a twelve-year-old inmate of a juvenile hall who habitually disrupted classes through constant talking and other undisciplined behavior. When he behaved this way, he was usually sent to his room. Lately, however, he had refused to stay there and it had become necessary to lock him in. His response to being locked up was to bang against the door with his fists and feet. The staff responded by placing him in the isolation cell in the basement, but his continued banging could still be héard throughout the building. Richard Fisch was called in by the staff to do something about the boy's uncontrollable behavior. Viewing the problem as one of interaction between the inmates and the authorities, Fisch reframed the situation by suggesting a game to the other children: everybody was to guess exactly how long Joe would continue his banging, and the one with the closest guess would be rewarded with a soda. Once all had made their guesses, one of the boys sneaked out of the classroom, ran to the window of the isolation cell, and shouted, "Joe, keep it up for another seven minutes, and I win a bottle of Coke!" The banging stopped immediately.

In dynamic terms, this resolution of the problem was similar to Jesus' healing of demoniacs: both involved mobilizing negative forces to achieve positive ends. Fisch does not appeal to the boy's best instincts but to his worst ones. The last thing Joe wants to do is to help another boy win the prize. So the reframing involves mobilizing his resistance to positive change in such a way as to effect this very alteration. Joe plays directly into Richard Fisch's hands. It is striking, too, how little Fisch needs to do, overtly, to effect this change. Like Jesus, who stands by as the demons thrust themselves into the herd of swine, Fisch sets a process in motion, and then watches it unfold.

CONCLUSION

These illustrations from Jesus' teaching and healing ministries tell us a number of important things about reframing. First, we need to identify the frame through which the counselee has viewed the situation up to this point. If we misperceive or misunderstand the original frame, our search for a viable reframing is quite impossible. If we cannot determine how the situation is being viewed, we cannot expect to be able to find ways to view it differently. Identifying the original frame—the meaning that the person ascribes to the situation—is an essential first step in the process of reframing.

Second, most situations may be framed in more than one way. As we saw with the parable of the two sons who were asked to work in the field, this episode could have been framed differently from the way that Jesus actually did it. This observation should put us on guard against assuming that similar situations will lend themselves to the same reframing. Reframings cannot be generalized. A reframing that succeeded in one situation may not work in another, similar case: "You can't reframe anything to anything else. It has to be something which fits that person's experience."[5] This clarification explains why it is impossible to characterize Jesus' healing method. Each healing is unique unto itself. Where other healers of his day (doctors and priests) used set formulas, Jesus improvised on the basis of the situation before him. We can take what we have learned from a successful or unsuccessful reframing and draw lessons from it, but we dare not take a successful reframing and merely apply it to a new situation. This is why reframing is not a science, which repeats the same procedures in analogous situations, but an art, where each situation is thoroughly unique. An art that merely repeats itself is not art.

Third, small, seemingly insignificant alterations in the prevailing system can produce dramatic changes. Jesus was impatient with elaborate designs for effecting change. An elaborate reframing plan may have its place, but Jesus preferred to do no more than was necessary to achieve the desired change. There was an economy of energy—both mental and physical—in his interventions. Similarly, we should focus our attention on those features of a dynamic system that are most amenable to change, and disregard the features that are so resistant as to require a very elaborate reframing plan. The point is not that reframing plans are to be avoided, but that simpler plans are preferable to elaborate ones. A small alteration in a dynamic system can produce a massive reorganization of the total system.

Fourth, there are times when counselees will formulate their own reframings. Usually, reframing comes at the initiative of the therapist, but on occasion, the counselee prescribes the plan before the therapist has had opportunity or reason to propose one. There is no problem with this. There were times when Jesus took the initiative in the reframing process (as in the case of the man who had lain beside the pool at Bethzatha for many years), and other times when the initiative was taken by the individual in need of help (as in the case of the woman who conceived the plan to touch

Jesus' garment as he passed by). In any given situation, the initiative for reframing depends on the circumstances and the resources of the individuals involved. However, the therapist has special responsibility for maintaining a clear distinction between an idea which is simply "more of the same" and a genuine reframing. Unlike the counselee, the therapist is aware of the difference, and has a responsibility to act on the basis of this awareness or knowledge.

Fifth, the parables and the healing stories of Jesus can be very useful for stimulating pastors' imaginations for their own reframings. Reframing theorists often illustrate the method with folktales, stories, and historical anecdotes. These stories help them keep their own imaginations alive and creative, and are often the inspiration for a particular reframing in the counseling setting. Jesus' parables and healings can serve a similar function in the pastor's use of reframing. Concrete illustrations of how the parables may contribute to such reframings are provided in the cases presented in the next two chapters.

CHAPTER FOUR
Superficial Counsel— A Case Study

The best way to demonstrate the value of any therapeutic method is with actual case illustrations. Through such examples we can see in what ways and to what extent a therapeutic method works. We can also test the method in our imaginations by picturing ourselves using it to see how it fits our own personal style of relating to other people. To demonstrate the value of reframing for pastoral care and counseling, I have chosen two cases in which reframing was not attempted, so that readers may see how the case would normally have gone. Then, in my discussion of the case, I show how the reframing method could have been utilized, and provide a rationale for the recommended reframing.

A CASE OF UNREQUITED OBLIGATION

Our first case is from Jay E. Adams's *The Use of the Scriptures in Counseling*.[1] This is one of four examples he uses to illustrate his approach to scriptural counseling. He entitles this case "Empathy," but I call it "A Case of Unrequited Obligation." Here is Adams's synopsis of the conversation which took place between the pastor and the counselee:

> "My situation is so different," Laurie explained. Laurie, the wife of a young seminarian, had come (she said) because "I feel obligated to David to keep working, since I want him to be able to

concentrate on school. I would never forgive myself if I quit my job, because he would have to reduce his class load in order to work, and I know that he wouldn't get as much out of school. But Pastor, I tell you, my job is impossible! I can't advance because I'm pegged as being temporary. I can't tell David or he'll tell me to quit. Less qualified men are promoted before me because, as my boss seemed happy to explain, 'a man's voice on the phone commands more respect, and therefore, is more valuable to the company.' And to top it off, I get no encouragement in the work that I am doing. I am losing my self-confidence; what shall I do?"

Adams, speaking for the counselor, adds: "Laurie's story tugs at your heart; not long ago you and your wife were in nearly an identical situation. You can empathize with her and are inclined to advise her that she might change jobs at the earliest opportunity. But you are not sure. 'Is there more that can be done for Laurie?' you wonder."

Adams provides his own analysis of the case. Since the example appears in his book on the use of the Bible in counseling, his analysis centers on scriptural passages which he considers relevant to Laurie's difficulties:

> In this case there are many features that might be emphasized. Let me quickly run through these. First, when Laurie says, "My situation is so different," the counselor, properly identifying with her, might have referred to 1 Corinthians 10:13, KJV ("No temptation has overtaken you that is not common to man"), quoting and explaining the verse, and powerfully concluding with a reference to his own experience. In part, her despair and her evident self-pity grew from her false, unbiblical notion that no one else had ever had to grapple with the difficulties with which she was struggling. The same verse also could be used to deal with her language which indicates that she has convinced herself that the situation is hopeless (cf. words of exaggeration—"never," "impossible"—and of impossibility—"can't," etc.).

Here, Adams recommends that the counselor refer to 1 Corinthians 10:13 to show Laurie that her situation is not as unique as she seems to think it is. Having established this point, the counselor should move to the matter of Laurie's relationship with David:

> Secondly, 1 Peter 3 in general is apropos concerning her submission to her husband. She is already involved in a deception

that could lead to serious marital communication problems. She first should have talked to him about her problem, and she should not have prejudged his reaction (in the actual case, he did not respond as she supposed). More specifically, by not telling him, she has made it difficult for him to exercise his responsibility to live with her "according to knowledge" (1 Peter 3:7, KJV). She must be willing to reveal all such matters that deeply influence them jointly so that he can fulfill his obligation to understand her.

Then there is the matter of her work situation. The counselor needs to address this, but should not take the approach that he initially considered (i.e., to suggest that she find another job at her earliest opportunity).

Lastly, somewhere in this session, Laurie needs to be confronted with the biblical work ethic found at the end of the third chapter of Colossians. A Christian does not work for her boss's acclaim, nor merely for earthly rewards. "It is the Lord Christ" whom she serves. And it is the same Christ who will acknowledge her faithfulness: "Well done, you good, faithful servant."

Adams' approach here is to convince Laurie to make some changes. She needs to act as a wife who is in "subjection" to her husband (1 Peter 3:1), by talking things over with him instead of trying to solve her problems on her own. Her well-intentioned effort to protect David from her problems, so that he can concentrate on his school work, actually undermines his role as her husband. She should also be more "faithful" to the biblical work ethic by viewing herself as a servant of Christ and not working for her boss's acclaim or for a promotion. As Colossians 3:23-24 puts it, "Whatever your task, work heartily, as serving the Lord and not men, knowing that from the Lord you will receive the inheritance as your reward. You are serving the Lord Christ."

Unfortunately for our purposes here, there are some missing facts in this case. For instance, we do not know how David actually responded when Laurie told him about her problem. We know his response was not what she expected, but we are not told what it was. The lack of this information hampers our analysis of the actual case and our proposal of a reframing plan. On the other hand, we know enough to assess Adams's recommended approach to the case and to offer an alternative based on reframing theory.

At first glance, Adams appears to offer a reframing. Laurie wonders if she should quit her job because it has become so meaningless to her. What's the point of working hard if you cannot receive some rewards for it? By introducing the Colossians passage, Adams invites her to look at her situation in a different light: "As a Christian, you are not working for your boss or even for yourself. You are working for Christ, and your reward is the inheritance that the Lord provides." Isn't this a reframing?

Superficially, it is. But because all the known facts are not taken into consideration, it is not a true reframing. Note, for example, that Laurie's concern at being passed over for promotions is only part of the problem. Even more troubling for her is her loss of self-confidence because "I get no encouragement in the work that I am doing." Adams does not address the erosion of her self-esteem, and fails to indicate how the perception that she is working for Christ, and not for herself or for others, will enable her to recover her sense of self-worth. Because known facts are being ignored, Adams has not provided a bona fide reframing.

Nor is his recommendation for change based on an adequate understanding of the original frame. He seems to view this frame as something like "working for rewards." But Laurie's understanding of the situation—the meaning which she ascribes to it—is much more self-involving and a great deal less utilitarian than is implied by the frame, "working for rewards." Instead, the frame is *unrequited obligation.* Laurie feels obligations to her husband and to her work, but receives little satisfaction and encouragement in return. Her need for reward or even approval are not inordinate. Rather, her sense of obligation to others is not adequately reciprocated. She feels this very clearly in her work situation where others, especially her boss, have the power and resources to provide encouragement but fail to do so. It is less clear whether David is failing her in this regard, but from the way that she talks about David and his seminary education, it is quite obvious that she feels a great deal of obligation to him. In telling the counselor that she is losing her self-esteem, the unverbalized but clearly implicit question she is asking, both of the counselor and of herself, is this: "Is anyone obligated to me?"

If unrequited obligation is the frame of Laurie's situation, then the inadequacy of Adams's prescription is all the more apparent. The 1 Peter 3 passage is used to pressure Laurie to talk about her problem with David, thus increasing the sense of obligation that she already feels toward him. It offers a first-order change—"more of the same"—when a second-order change is needed. The same assessment applies to the Colossians passage, which merely reinforces her frame of obligation. This biblical reference charges her with the obligation to "work heartily" because this is what is expected of a Christian. Thus, added to her sense of obligation to her employer and her husband, she is now also obligated to Christ—even though he announced his ministry as proclaiming release to the captives (Luke 4:18-19). If she were to read the Colossians passage on her own and to find some encouragement in it, this would be one thing. But for the counselor to use it to admonish her to go back to her job and throw herself into her work changes nothing. The very fact that Laurie has come to the counselor for help tells us that changes in her obligation frame are needed. But, if she were to take the counselor's advice, as based on 1 Peter 3 and Colossians 3, she would discover that the more things change, the more they remain the same. Her life still would be oriented to her obligation to others, and nothing would have been done about her sense of injustice or her loss of self-confidence.

Obviously, recent events at work have begun to challenge the adequacy of the obligation frame as a way of life. Her sense of obligation is not being reciprocated. Her boss feels no corresponding obligation to treat her fairly. He uses her gender, and its alleged characteristics (i.e., a less "commanding" voice), as grounds for depriving her of promotions that are rightfully hers. It is not that she has an inordinate need for her boss's "acclaim," as Adams suggests. Instead, she wants, and has a right to expect, simple equity and fairness. She is the victim of unrequited obligation.

Of course, we should not ignore the fact that a reason given for her boss's failure to promote her was that she was considered a temporary employee. We might have viewed this as a fair and just basis for her not being promoted, except that, by her boss's own admission, it was not the sole reason. The other equally if not more influential reason was that she was a woman. What a dubious rationale for the decision to promote less-qualified persons ahead of her. Still, that she was viewed as being temporary is an important fact for the counselor to keep in mind when formulating a reframing plan.

What about her married life? We don't know, from the facts provided, whether David reciprocated her sense of obligation. But we *do* know that he did not respond as she expected when she informed him about her difficulties at work. Whatever he said to her, it was not to advise her to quit her present job. Apparently, he agreed with Adams that the solution was not to quit, but his rationale for doing so is unclear. As a seminarian intending to go into the ordained ministry, maybe he shared Adams's views regarding the "biblical work ethic." Perhaps he cited one or another pragmatic reason for her to remain in her current job, such as their financial situation, or the impermanence of her position, because of which she should try to hold out "just a little longer." Or maybe he used the very argument that she herself offered for not quitting—that he would have to reduce his course load if he were to take a job. If he did advance this argument, we need not assume that he necessarily presented it in a self-serving way ("I came here to study for the ministry and this is what I intend to do"). He could just as well have noted that if he were to take a job, they would prolong their stay at seminary. In any event, we may assume that his advice was based either on a theological principle ("biblical work ethic") or on pragmatic considerations, neither of which would take account of the erosion of Laurie's self-esteem. Has David no obligation to her to see that she does not suffer a negative change in self-image as a consequence of their life together? Is David's obliviousness to her loss of self-esteem any less sinful than her boss's overt mistreatment?

We conclude that the frame within which Laurie was acting out her life was the frame of obligation, and that this frame had become self-destructive. A reframing, designed to achieve second-order change, was essential. The question is how to achieve it. Obviously, any effective reframing would acknowledge her attempts at certain solutions which had not been successful. She had talked with her boss about his failure to promote her, but had received no satisfactory explanation. She had talked to David, but he had not reacted as she had anticipated. Thus, efforts to discuss the problem with the persons involved in her obligation frame had not produced satisfactory results. While this approach had seemed to make sense, it had not achieved anything. The fact that she had talked about her situation with her boss and her husband had only increased her sense of obligation, placing her in a double bind. The more things changed, the more they remained the same.

A different approach is needed, and here I agree with Adams that the alternative approach is not for Laurie to quit her job—not, at least, until she has tried another alternative, one based on reframing theory. This alternative approach would build upon the fact that her present job is a temporary one. She does not feel that she should quit her job, but neither does she view it as a long-term commitment. Thus, this job offers a setting in which she may experiment with her sense of obligation in ways that she may be unwilling to do in her marriage, which she views as a lasting commitment, or in a subsequent job, which she may view as more permanent. The reframing would focus, in other words, on her work situation, and, more specifically, on her freedom, as a temporary employee, to experiment with her sense of obligation in new and different ways.

How would this new scenario work? What would be a viable reframing plan? Recall that reframing may be achieved through a seemingly minor behavioral change. The case of the restaurant owners is a good example. Arranging for the husband to arrive a half hour earlier than the wife made a noticeable difference in their working relationship. Another good example is the case of the dental assistant who was afraid she would be fired for making a big mistake. For her, reframing meant deliberately making a small, inconsequential error every day. Forced to concentrate her thoughts on devising and carrying through on this small error, she found she was unable to make the big mistake that she had feared she would commit; it was hard enough to make a small error.

In a similar way, Laurie's situation might be reframed if each week she deliberately made one or two mistakes which would cause the organization, under her boss's leadership, to function less effectively. This action might involve her "inexplicably" omitting some significant details from a report she has been asked to prepare; or "losing" a document that provides some information about a project which is under consideration; or "forgetting" to relay valuable information to her boss or one of the men he has promoted ahead of her. Each mistake would be sufficiently unique and unpredictable that her boss would not easily recognize a set pattern of irresponsibility. The mistakes would not be so blatant or of such great magnitude that he would have grounds for firing her, or even for issuing warnings or severe reprimands. They would be minor, yet significant irritants, causes for confusion or work disruption— enough to give her some sense of avenging the wrongs that have been done to her. Also, these mistakes should not be ones that would make her own life more difficult. Instead, they should complicate life for her boss and his colleagues but, more important, enable her to feel that her boss has lost effective power or control over her. He can deprive her of the promotions that she deserves, but she has the power to complicate his life and undermine his power to break her spirit.

Her ability to exercise this power will provide new grounds for self-confidence. No longer basing her self-esteem solely on her ability to please the persons she works for, she will find that there must be other, more intrinsic sources of self-confidence. Instead of being grounded in her ability to do better work than others, and on the encouragement that she hopes to receive from this, her self-confidence will have its basis in her capacity to exercise control over her own life, irrespective of the encouragement she receives from others.

Adams's approach to this case is supported by certain biblical texts. I can also claim biblical support for my reframing plan. Specific psalms of lament support my diagnostic assessment of her situation, and the parable of the dishonest steward (Luke 16:1-8) suggests the proposed reframing. The lament psalms, especially Psalms 62, 64, and 86, help us to feel the pain that she experiences from the injustices inflicted upon her, and to empathize with the angry feelings such injustice evokes in her. This injustice is captured in the following verse from Psalm 86: "O God, insolent men have risen up against me; a band of ruthless men seek my life, and they do not set thee before them" (v. 14). The effects of such injustice on her self-esteem are captured in the following verse from Psalm 62: "How long will you set upon a [woman] to shatter [her], all of you, like a leaning wall, a tottering fence?" (v. 3).

Her boss's callous explanation for why she was passed over for promotion, and the helpless and vengeful feelings this evokes, is expressed in these verses from Psalm 64: "Hear my voice, O God, in my complaint; preserve my life from dread of the enemy, hide me from the secret plots of the wicked, from the scheming of evildoers, who whet their tongues like swords, who aim bitter words like arrows, shooting from ambush at the blameless, shooting at [her] suddenly and without fear" (vs. 1–4). These verses correctly identify the gross injustice of her boss's promotion of others ahead of her as "secret plots" and "scheming," and they accurately describe his explanation for this procedure as "bitter words" which, like arrows, are shot at her from his position of safety. Expressing anger at enemies who shoot off words from ambush, these verses also capture the unintended irony of the boss's assertion that "a man's voice commands more respect." His very words falsify this claim, for how can Laurie, or anyone else, respect a man who makes such an assertion? As the psalmist says, he could respect an enemy who comes out from his ambush and makes himself vulnerable to counterattack. But Laurie's boss sits behind his desk, throwing out cruel barbs—"a man's voice"—and she is helpless to do anything about it.

Short of the reframing plan offered here, what can she do? She can threaten to quit, and he will simply accept her resignation as legitimation of her transience and of his promotion strategy, and hire someone else. She can threaten to sue on the grounds of discrimination, but he will deny he ever said that he gives priority to men because they have deeper voices; he will instead say that Laurie was passed up for promotion because she was temporary. What she *can* do is what the reframing plan proposes: to ambush *him* through her own "secret plots." She will never be able to do to him what he has done to her, and she really does not want to. Why sink to his level? But she can and ought to avenge the injury that he has done to her self-esteem.

Some, of course, might argue that such avenging is wrong, and unbecoming of a Christian. Some argue that we should leave the avenging of wrongs to God (Rom. 12:19). But such feelings are common to the lament psalms, with God often called upon to help the psalmist avenge himself on his enemies. Thus, in Psalm 86, the psalmist pleads with God to "turn to me and take pity on me; give thy strength to thy servant, and save the son of thy handmaid. Show me a sign of thy favor, that those who hate me may see and be put to shame because thou, Lord, hast helped and comforted me" (vs. 116–17). Laurie has come to her pastor, seeking some way that her situation can be changed. She wants a sign of God's favor, some change in the situation that will restore her confidence. The proposed reframing is actually a rather mild plan for avenging herself on her enemies. Its purpose is not solely to gain revenge but to enable her to have a sense of power which she never experienced as long as she assumed that she was more obligated to others than they were to her. In this way, the reframing plan lays the groundwork for her to experience tokens of God's favor, especially in the form of renewed self-confidence. Thus, desires to avenge herself are not denied and are not considered unbecoming of a Christian. But they are not ends in themselves, either. Instead, they are used to motivate her to adopt the reframing plan, whose purpose is to enable her to regain her self-confidence, and to find a more adequate basis for self-esteem than the frame of obligation.

Thus, psalms of lament are extremely useful in assessing Laurie's situation, as they capture her sense of being under siege and hemmed in on every side. In a very poignant way, they express the feelings that she is experiencing, and enable the counselor to do a far better job of what Adams says this case is about: showing empathy. They sensitize us to Laurie's feelings of anger toward those who have injured her, and enable us to recognize desires, unverbalized but certainly present, to avenge herself. They help us to see that a reframing of her situation must take account of such feelings and desires, and to view them as not only understandable but thoroughly legitimate. Laurie is a victim of grave injustice, and the counselor has no right or reason to challenge these feelings, even if they include the desire to take revenge. The counselor, however, does have a responsibility to see that these desires are expressed in a way that is not counterproductive for Laurie nor clearly unethical. Knowing what we know about Laurie, her obligation frame, there is much greater danger that she will do something counter-productive for herself than that she will do something unethical. She may be quite reluctant to enact the proposed plan on the grounds that a Christian should not "return evil for evil." Maybe so. But neither should Christians allow others to break their spirits. Her boss can, and will, take care of himself. The question is whether Laurie can begin to take care of *herself* by nurturing the spirit which God has given her, and which is the ultimate source of genuine self-confidence.

Our second biblical support for the reframing plan is the parable of the dishonest steward (Luke 16:1-8):

There was a rich man who had a steward, and charges were brought to him that this man was wasting his goods. And he called him and said to him, "What is this that I hear about you? Turn in the account of your stewardship, for you can no longer be steward." And the steward said to himself, "What shall I do, since my master is taking the stewardship away from me? I am not strong enough to dig, and I am ashamed to beg. I have decided what to do, so that people may receive me into their houses when I am put out of the stewardship. So, summoning his master's debtors one by one, he said to the first, "How much do you owe my master?" He said, "A hundred measures of oil." And he said to him, "Take your bill, and sit down quickly and write fifty." Then he said to another, "And how much do you owe?" He said, "A hundred measures of wheat." He said to him, "Take your bill, and write eighty." The master commended the dishonest steward for his prudence; for the sons of this world are wiser in their own generation than the sons of light.

The parable doesn't fit Laurie's case in every detail, but there are significant parallels. Laurie, of course, has not been charged with wasting her master's goods or threatened with firing. But there is a conflict between her and her boss and the possibility of her termination has been considered. Moreover, in both situations there is the perception that the employee has been found wanting and is expendable. As a result, both are placed in difficult situations calling for creative response. The dishonest steward takes advantage of his one last task before he leaves his master's employ: the turning in of his accounts. He cleverly uses this remaining obligation to avenge his termination by placing himself in a more advantageous position after he is fired. The reframing plan proposed here takes similar advantage of the fact that Laurie, while passed over for promotion, is still employed; she is therefore still "obligated" to her employer and can make creative use of this situation. Through the reframing, this "obligation" will be turned to her advantage.

Also, as with the steward's case, the reframing plan recognizes the important long-term gains that will last beyond Laurie's present employment. The longer-range gains which Laurie will realize from the reframing plan will be permanent changes in her life frame (i.e., the frame of obligation), which will also result in permanent changes in her self-valuation. These changes will be based on her shift from a self-defeating frame of obligation to a self-invigorating frame of personal empowerment.

The parable ends with the master commending the steward for his prudence. I take it that Jesus is telling the "children of light" to develop such wisdom. Most likely, the reframing proposed in Laurie's case will not have a similar outcome, largely because her boss is not as perceptive as the steward's master and will probably not realize what Laurie is doing. But the steward's knowledge that his reframing will have positive consequences after he leaves his master's employ does apply directly to Laurie. By discovering that she has the power to create confusion and consternation for her boss and his allies, and to do so without bringing attention to herself, she will have learned that she is quite capable of counteracting the undermining of her self-confidence by others.

It is also noteworthy that even as the master did not condemn his steward, so Jesus, the storyteller, did not condemn him either. The steward's actions were questionable from a moral point of view, and yet Jesus praised him for his ingenuity. If Laurie were to have misgivings about the reframing plan being proposed here— the appropriateness for a Christian of "returning evil for evil"— the counselor might cite this parable as an example of Jesus' commendation of a worker who took shrewd personal advantage of a rather desperate situation, not unlike her own. Obviously, Laurie is not being encouraged to act unethically, and is emphatically not being advised to do anything that could possibly be construed as meant for her own personal gain. Nor should her "mistakes" cause innocent persons to suffer. As in the parable, the idea is not that she will cause irreparable harm to anyone, but only discomfort and dismay for the person and his allies who have treated her shamefully. If Jesus can commend the dishonest steward, whose actions were clearly unethical, then surely the reframing plan for Laurie is not unchristian. On the contrary, what *is* unchristian is to allow others to break our spirits, to let them reduce our existence to a living hell.

Thus, by using the parable of the dishonest steward to support the proposed reframing plan, my view of what it means to "work in service to Christ" is quite different from Adams's interpretation. In his view, service to Christ means that Laurie is to accept the injustices inflicted upon her, to put aside thoughts of earthly reward, and to work instead for Christ's glory: "Whatever your task, work heartily, as serving the Lord and not men" (Col. 3:23). But the parable of the dishonest steward says that we glorify God by exhibiting a certain shrewdness in our dealings with those whom we have reason to mistrust. Why is it, Jesus asks, that the children of this world are wiser than the children of light? By developing a certain shrewd wisdom in her relations with her boss, Laurie will in fact give glory to God. It was not unwise for her to go to her boss initially to learn why she had been passed over for promotion. But now a different approach is needed, one that is less direct, one that is, quite frankly, more subversive. The promotion that is rightfully hers will not be achieved through this reframing. But in adopting this approach, she will be acting constructively on her own lament—"I am losing my self-confidence"— and also on her Lord's lament: Why is it that the children of this world are wiser than the children of light?

CONCLUSION

I do not know Laurie personally and have no biographical information about her, so I have no way of knowing how she might respond to this proposed reframing. Maybe the real Laurie would respond more favorably to the pastoral intervention advocated by Adams (though I have not encountered a woman yet who did not find his proposal offensive). On the other hand, maybe my counterproposal is impractical for the real Laurie, who might view it as unbecoming of a Christian (and seminarian's wife), or simply find that being somewhat "irresponsible" is not within her behavioral repertoire, being a violation of everything for which she stands. Or maybe she would object that the plan is actually too weak, and not direct enough. In that case, a different attempt at reframing would be necessary. As we have seen, reframings are situation-specific: "You have to find a valid set of perceptions in terms of that particular person's model of the world."[2] To test this proposed reframing empirically, I presented it to my introductory class in pastoral care and counseling and found that only three of the forty seminarians would be willing to propose it to Laurie. A number of students said that it reflected an "Old Testament ethic" in which avenging the wrongs committed against oneself was considered appropriate, but that this ethic has been superseded by the Christian ethic which is based on love, including love for one's enemies. But when I asked these students how they would then reframe the situation, taking more adequate account of the love ethic, they were uncertain or vague as to what such a reframing would be. This uncertainty does not discredit the argument that the students were making, but neither does it do the Lauries of this world much good. It does not acknowledge that no Christian ethic worthy of the name takes justice any less seriously than love. A number of the students who had voted against the reframing plan proposed here stated that they had done something rather similar in their own work experiences, and some even admitted that, on hindsight, they wished they had done it more often.

It should also be noted that reframing plans are always subject to review. Were a counselor to recommend this plan, one or more visits with Laurie would certainly be arranged in order to evaluate it. My hope is that it would not only help Laurie regain the self-confidence she had lost, but would also provide a new basis for it. She would discover that her worth as a person is not based on her capacity to be an obligated, obliging individual. But it is possible that the plan would not have this intended effect, and for this reason, would need to be replaced with a different plan. Reframing plans are not set in concrete. They are always subject to review and evaluation. Also, in this particular instance, the reframing plan is sufficiently flexible (e.g., as to the number of mistakes Laurie would need to make within a given time frame) that much of the initiative for implementing it remains with her.

I acknowledge that the real Laurie might not only dismiss the reframing plan proposed here, but might also question the ability and the integrity of the counselor, and take her leave. Even if this were to happen, I would feel better about having offered her a new "frame," based on the lament psalms and the parable of the dishonest steward, than having tried to reinforce her existing "frame" on the basis of 1 Peter 3 and Colossians 3. I do not suggest that the 1 Peter and Colossians texts are inherently inferior to the others. I mean only that they are used by Adams to reinforce

Laurie's existing frame. They are thus used in violation of the Christian gospel which, as our earlier discussion of Jesus' parables and healings revealed, is fundamentally committed to reframing. The Colossians text challenges us to "work heartily in service to Christ." I claim that the reframing plan would make this challenge a reality for Laurie. I also contend that pastoral counselors who use the art of reframing have a greater sense of "working heartily in service to Christ" than those who resist its use.

CHAPTER FIVE
Healing Utopia— A Case Study

Our next case focuses on a very common situation confronted by parish pastors, one which is usually handled through informal pastoral care interventions rather than formal counseling. This is the problem of tensions and conflicts between parents and their teenage children. Sometimes these conflicts are severe enough to prompt the pastor to recommend formal counseling. Often, however, they are treated informally, as part of the pastor's ongoing relationship to the family. This case shows that reframing can be used effectively in informal pastoral care. Because it involves a teenager, the case also demonstrates that reframing may be used with any age group. In fact, reframing can be especially effective with teenagers because it does not require sustained or long-term counseling.

This case also enables us to explore a perplexing question in pastoral care: How do we determine when second-order change is indicated? Many pastors would treat this as a case in which first-order change only is required: the need for adjustments—nothing more dramatic. Yet, the pastoral care of teenagers is often frustrating and unrewarding because first-order change is sought where second-order change is needed. It is neither the severity of the problem nor the maturity of the person experiencing the problem that indicates the appropriateness of second-order change. Indeed, many situations involving teenagers are not severe at first; they become so precisely because first-order changes were attempted, compounding the problem.

A CASE OF INCREDIBLE AMBITION

This case involves Andy McCallister, a fifteen-year-old boy, and Carl Jensen, a young associate minister who was somewhat a role-model for Andy. Carl was responsible for the youth program of the church, which was located in downtown Minneapolis. Andy's parents were very involved in the church and he was quite active in the youth group. Andy's father noted that Carl had not talked with Andy for some time, and felt it might be good for him to do so, since Andy looked up to him. Later, Mrs. McCallister made comments suggesting that Andy had some personal problems which Carl might be able to help him resolve. She mentioned that Andy had been physically ill, but that the doctor couldn't find anything wrong with him. She surmised that he hated school and was trying to avoid it by pretending to be sick. She also mentioned to Carl that Andy had expressed the desire to transfer to another high school, one that had a strong program in theater, because he had decided he wanted to become an actor. She felt that this rather sudden decision had something to do with Andy's budding relationship with Jody, a girl who attended their church and was already enrolled in the theater arts program at the other high school. Mrs. McCallister told Carl that she had tried to dissuade Andy from considering a career in acting because it would be so difficult. She left the clear impression that she hoped Carl would try to reinforce what she had been saying to Andy, using his influence with her son to try to redirect his career decision.

With these signals from the parents, Carl phoned Andy and suggested they meet at a local fast-food restaurant after school. Andy was willing to do so, and the meeting was arranged. Before it took place, Mr. McCallister mentioned to Carl that Andy had asked him whether his parents had suggested this visit, and whether they had done so to enlist Carl's aid in discouraging him from an acting career. Mr. McCallister had acknowledged mentioning to Carl that it would be good for the two of them to get together. He also said that as far as he was concerned, there was no hidden agenda and no expectations placed on Carl to take any position. Whether he was aware of Mrs. McCallister's conversations with

Carl, in which such expectations were clearly expressed, we do not know. As Andy and Carl settled into the restaurant booth the following conversation ensued:

CARL: So how's school going?
ANDY: Great! I like school. It won't be long until I'll be going to college.
CARL: What do you think you're interested in?
ANDY: I don't know. [Pause] I like to act. I want to go to Jackson High, where I can major in theater arts.
CARL: You do?
ANDY: Yeah, but you know you have to audition to get in. My parents are going to see about getting me voice lessons.
CARL: So you'd audition by singing?
ANDY: Yeah, maybe. Singing or acting. Jody goes there and she's going to help me with acting after church. She knows all about it.
CARL: Jody?
ANDY: Yeah, Jody Fjetland. You know the girl at the church who was in the Homecoming production?
CARL: Oh, yeah. She's a pretty girl.
ANDY: She's perfect! She does it all—sings, dances, acts. And she's beautiful!

Andy then said that Jody had just broken up with a twenty-one-year-old man who was an actor and model, and that Jody's mother liked Andy because she felt he was a good influence for her, unlike Jody's other friends. Andy noted that his parents had not discouraged his relationship with Jody, but did indicate that they were "worried about her virginity." The conversation continued:

CARL: Maybe you can be a good influence on her.
ANDY: She's doing fine. She quit smoking yesterday. I told her she didn't want black lungs.
CARL: Well, that's good. [Pause] So what's the game plan as far as going to Jackson High is concerned?
ANDY: Well, I'll be taking my voice lessons soon. And I'm in a drama class in school. My teacher says I have a lot of talent.

CARL: You know, I never realized you liked performing so much.

ANDY: Sure. Remember I did the play at church? And I've done some school plays.

CARL: Well, I don't have to tell you how tough a career it is.

ANDY: I know. My parents don't want me to do it. They say it's too hard.

CARL: Well, Andy, if you are interested in it, you ought to try to get some good training. It's good you're going to start taking voice lessons.

They chatted a while longer about other topics, then left the restaurant and got back into the car. As they were driving to Andy's house, the following conversation took place:

CARL: So you're pretty satisfied with how things are going for you?

ANDY: I guess so. I don't know why I shouldn't be.

CARL: So when would you start the singing lessons?

ANDY: I don't know. [Long pause] You know, it's funny. My parents really don't want me to. I mean, after I did that play two years ago at church, my parents were complimenting me and everything and saying like, I have this talent, and if they could do anything to help me follow up on it, they'd help me and stuff like that, and now that I want to, they can't.

CARL: Maybe they think that you're partly doing it because of Jody.

ANDY: Yeah, that's what I think they think. But I wanted to even before I did anything with Jody.

CARL: So you think that if someone else had given you the information about the school, besides Jody, you'd be just as up for it?

ANDY: I probably would. I think I would be.

CARL: Well, then, try for it, and let's see what happens.

ANDY: My parents keep telling me stuff like how hard it is, how my brother had to learn Italian. [Imitating his parents:] "It's so hard, Andy, I'm not sure you want to do this." [Answering them back:] "Shut up!" They're just trying to discourage me so bad!

Just then, they arrived at Andy's house and he jumped out of the car. Carl accompanied him into the house, talked briefly with other members of the family, and then left.

In his analysis of this case, Carl felt that he had done more to encourage than discourage Andy. But he also expressed his belief that Andy probably wouldn't be pursuing acting very long. This idea was based partly on Andy's youth, and partly on the knowledge that many of us do not follow the vocational directions we consider at age fifteen. Also, when Andy was asked what he was interested in, he responded, "I don't know." Only after a pause did he say he wanted to be an actor. The uncertainty in his response seems to support Carl's intuitive sense that Andy might well shift to another career choice if he were not made to feel defensive about it by his parents. A third reason for Carl's feeling that Andy would not become an actor was his sense that Andy suffered from low self-esteem; his desire to go into acting probably had much to do with his need to boost his self-confidence. This, in Carl's view, created a paradox. "Since there is so much rejection in this field [theater], it can become a nightmare for someone with low self-esteem. The device that fed Andy's self-esteem by telling him how good he is will start to take away from it by telling him how bad he is. If Andy does decide to pursue acting, I think the rejection factor will force him to stop."

This is a case in which reframing is indicated. To be sure, based upon how the case was actually handled, this choice does not appear to be obvious. Carl does not approach the case as though it requires reframing. His major concern is to be supportive of Andy; at the same time, he wants to encourage him to be realistic. If Andy really wants to pursue an acting career, he needs to prepare himself for it now and he needs to be aware of the pitfalls and risks. These concerns all fall within the domain of first-order change. There is no systematic attempt to reframe the situation, no intentional effort to get Andy to look at the matter from a radically different perspective.

What are the grounds, it might be asked, for my assertion that an intentional effort to reframe the situation is needed? There are two reasons which prompt my claim for reframing. First, Andy himself feels caught in a double bind: his parents had earlier encouraged his interest in acting, now they are warning him of its dangers. First-order change efforts, like those attempted by the parents, have done nothing to resolve this double bind; they have only increased it. Second, the solutions already attempted by Andy's parents do not appear to be working. His parents' attempts to dissuade him from an acting career because it is too difficult have only embittered Andy against them: "They're just trying to discourage me so bad." Also, their efforts to involve Carl in persuading Andy to alter his course have caused Andy to become more suspicious. The attempted solutions have not produced results and actually seem to be making the problem worse. Therefore, second-order change through reframing is not only appropriate, it is the most viable option available.

How would such a reframing proceed? Given Mr. and Mrs. McCallister's unproductive efforts in persuading Andy to think more realistically and to consider the extreme difficulty of an acting career, Carl could take the opposite tack. In his next conversation with Andy, he could observe that Andy's desire to become an actor is all right as far as it goes, but that a person with his obvious gifts should be thinking much more ambitiously. He should be planning a future which is somehow grander, more visionary, more reflective of a free and unrestrained imagination! In other words, is Andy being visionary enough? Or is he thinking too narrowly? Is he being too pragmatic, too down-to-earth, and not idealistic enough?

If Andy were to feel that Carl, in saying this, was only trying to encourage him to consider another career—a subtle putdown of his desire to become an actor—the appropriate and honest response would be, "No, that's not what I meant. I'm not saying that some other career is necessarily better than the one you're thinking about. It's just that, from where I sit, you seem to be so darned practical about it all. You aren't letting yourself dream big. It's not the acting thing that bothers me. It's the fact that you seem so constrained, like you have to stay within set limits."

If Carl took this approach, he would be acting on his suspicion that Andy may decide, in the end, not to pursue an acting career, and that he may be pressing for it because his parents have put him on the defensive. But Carl would not be trying to dissuade Andy from this choice for the reasons that his parents have voiced (i.e., that acting may be "too difficult" for him), reasons that Andy has appropriately rejected. Nor would he be questioning Andy's motives for wanting to become an actor, as Andy suspects his parents are doing, by attributing this sudden desire to his interest in Jody. Instead, Carl would be acting on his perception that Andy's self-esteem is what is truly at issue here. Andy's self-confidence, fragile to begin with, is being weakened even more by his mother's warnings against a career that would be so hard for him. Contrary to his parents' approach, Carl would be questioning whether Andy is being too practical, too narrowly goal-oriented, too constrained in his thinking, and not idealistic enough. Carl would be coming at the issue from a perspective diametrically opposite that of Andy's parents.

This reframing would be similar to the one proposed by Watzlawick, Weakland, and Fisch in dealing with utopias:

> Common sense suggests that the best way of dealing with problems arising from exaggerated goals is by pointing to their practical flaws and absurdities in the hope that the utopian will then see them. As is almost the rule in human problems, common-sense solutions are the most self-defeating and sometimes even the most destructive ones. To try to inject "reality" into utopias establishes and maintains a first-order change impasse through the introduction of the reciprocal member (i.e., common sense vs. utopianism).[1]

So how does the therapist pursue the goal of second-order change in this case?

> A person with very high-flying goals in life will not take kindly to any attempt to convince him to scale down his plans and to make them more realistic. For him this is nothing but an invitation to resign himself to a miserable, depressing way of living; therefore the language of common sense is the least appropriate or successful in dealing with him. What he does understand, only too well, is the language of utopia. Of course, common sense balks at the idea of feeding into, rather than opposing, that which needs to be changed. But we have already seen that the way to deal with a pessimist is to outdo his pessimism, and, analogously, the utopian will usually relinquish his utopias most quickly if they are taken beyond his own limits.[2]

To illustrate, the authors cite the case of a twenty-nine-year-old schizophrenic who had grandiose plans for himself, including studying the sitar under Ravi Shankar so that his music would influence the Western world and, at the same time, studying Chinese agricultural methods to feed the globe's starving masses. "When the therapist agreed with these goals in principle but found them not sufficiently big, the patient countered this by beginning to talk about a far less ambitious plan, namely to get involved in a halfway house." To this more practical proposal, the therapist responded that the idea of getting into a halfway house "is all right in its place, but to keep your mind that much on the practical is certain to constrain you in using your imagination to get to a higher level and to think in larger and more comprehensive terms." To this the patient replied: "Every time I go to a higher level, it is more abstract. It takes time and I don't have any—I'm out of, you know—these big, practical problems I am haunted by, you know, like I have to—I have run out of money and I have to get something immediately—that's the problem." The authors conclude: "By consistently using this technique the therapist was able to bring the dialogue down to more and more practical levels."[3]

Obviously, the twenty-nine-year-old schizophrenic has ideas that are far more grandiose than Andy's, and there is nothing pathological in a teenager's aspiring to become an actor. But Andy's case is similar in that his parents view his desire to be an actor as utopian; they are responding with common-sense efforts to deal with his "exaggerated goals" by pointing out their practical flaws and absurdities. This approach is not working. All it does is invite Andy "to resign himself to a miserable, depressing way of living." As he says, "They're just trying to discourage me so bad." Therefore, the hope for a second-order change lies in a different direction. It involves picking up where his apparently exaggerated or utopian goals leave off and taking them a step further. It is not that his plans are grandiose, but that they may be too limited and modest.

What might happen if Carl were to reframe the situation this way? From the case of the twenty-nine-year-old schizophrenic, we would anticipate that Andy would begin to look at the situation in a more practical manner. He might counter Carl's observation by affirming that a person has to be practical and realistic, he has to look at his life in a mature way. If Carl persisted in challenging this line of thinking, continuing to argue for dreaming large dreams and daring to pursue them, Andy might counter by examining an acting career, noting its pluses and minuses, and expressing his own reservations about it without any prodding from Carl. Whatever course the conversation might take, it would not involve urging Andy to be practical and sensible about the whole matter—a role that pastors, often to their great frustration, frequently find themselves adopting. When did Jesus ever counsel a commonsensical approach to human dilemmas?

To some, this proposed reframing may appear to be manipulative and insincere. The pastor seems to be playing a game with Andy, and relating to him in a less-than-honest and straightforward manner. But is this approach any more insincere than Carl's actual proposal that Andy get some good acting training even as he harbors the suspicion that Andy is unlikely to become an actor? Also, and more important, there is something profoundly true in the suggestion that Andy take a more expansive view of his life and its possibilities. In his analysis of the case, Carl noted that Isaiah 40:29-31 is especially relevant to Andy's situation:

> He gives power to the faint,
>> and to him who has no might he increases strength.
> Even youths shall faint and be weary,
>> and young men shall fall exhausted;
> but they who wait for the Lord
>> shall renew their strength,
> They shall mount up with wings like eagles,
>> They shall run and not be weary,
> They shall walk and not faint.

By viewing Andy's situation from the perspective of these verses, Carl perceived that his role was not to discourage Andy from envisioning great things for himself. To do so would be to deny the power of God to increase the strength of those who have no might, to imply that God's power has no real efficacy in situations like Andy's, to believe that Andy's case needs to be viewed according to a realistic appraisal of his abilities. On sound biblical grounds, Carl rejects these implications. Yet his counseling of Andy reflects them. The reframing method does not.

Thus, on the basis of Carl's own biblical citation, our proposed reframing is thoroughly appropriate. To encourage Andy to take a more expansive view of his life, to permit his imagination and dreams to run freely, is consistent with the assurance contained in this passage from Isaiah that youths who wait upon the Lord shall mount up with wings like eagles. There is nothing inherently manipulative or deceitful in this reframing. If Andy responds by marshaling arguments for approaching his future career in a more practical way than he has done before, there is some value in this outcome; it will arrest the trend toward greater conflict between Andy and his parents. On the other hand, if he takes the reframing proposal at face value and imagines an even more glorious future for himself than he has dared to consider so far, this, too, will be entirely acceptable and welcome. Either way, the counseling process has broken through the impasse created by the application of common-sense solutions to what were perceived to be unrealistic aspirations.

A parable which captures Andy's sense of being put in an untenable bind by his parents is the parable of the marriage feast (Matt. 22:1-14). It tells that a king prepared a marriage feast for his son, but the invited guests refused to come. Instead, they killed the servants whom the king sent to invite them. He retaliated by sending his troops to destroy the murderers and burn their city. Then he ordered his servants to go to the thoroughfares and invite as many people as they could find so that the wedding hall would be filled with guests. When he came in to look at the guests, however, he saw a man who had no wedding garment, and said to him, "Friend, how did you get in here without a wedding garment?" The man was speechless. Then the king ordered his attendants to throw the man out.

This parable is a classic example of the double bind. The king wanted to fill the wedding hall with guests so he invited everyone he could find. But then he turned on one of the guests for failing to wear the traditional wedding attire. This is the situation in which Andy finds himself. After he performed in a church play, his parents complimented him, said he had talent, and promised to do anything they could to help him develop it. Now that he wants to pursue this talent in a more extensive and committed way, his parents oppose the idea: "Now that I want to, they can't." Like the man who had come at the king's bidding, Andy had only done what his parents had encouraged him to do. Now that he is doing it, they are unhappy with the outcome. And how have they handled their unhappiness? They could have taken the honest approach of saying they regretted having encouraged him earlier. Instead, they point to difficulties which have emerged in the meantime that, to them, justify their change of heart. There's the matter of his brother's difficulty in learning Italian. And there's Jody. Yes, she goes to our church, but she smokes and her virginity is in doubt. Is this where your interest in acting is leading? Into the seductive arms of a girl of doubtful morality?

Andy, rightly, suspects that these arguments are self-serving and spurious. Once the king's problem of filling the wedding hall was solved, he worried that he had created a new dilemma for himself: "If the rabble in the wedding hall are my new constituency, my new supporters, what does this mean for my own personal status? How does this make me look—I who am accustomed to the presence of the finest, richest, most beautiful people in the land?" Thus, one hapless guest is taught that the king's standards are still in place, that he has not changed as a result of this social and political realignment. Likewise, Mr. and Mrs. McCallister experienced the problem common to parents of all teenagers: "Let's hope that Andy finds some interests in life, that he finds some constructive avenue for channeling his abilities and talents." In solving the first problem, however, they created another. Andy is now attracted to a profession which they cannot wholeheartedly endorse. How can they deal with this new problem? For the king in the parable, a flaw in the system is identified and used to discredit the system itself. He looks out on the sea of wedding guests and, lo, he discovers that one man came without the proper wedding attire. By making an example of him, the king will communicate to the whole crowd that nothing in his regime has fundamentally changed. For Andy's plans, the flaw has something to do with Jody. Because Andy has included her in his plans, everything can be called into question. The problem is not his parents and the mixed signals they have directed toward Andy. The problem is Jody. She is the equivalent of the man who failed to wear the proper attire to the wedding feast. She is the convenient instrument for initiating the trap of the double-bind.

If the parable of the wedding feast captures the bind in which Andy's parents have placed him, what parable supports our reframing? It is the parable of the mustard seed (Mark 4:30-32). Jesus asks, "To what can the kingdom of God be compared?" The answer, he suggests, is the mustard seed. It is the smallest of seeds but grows up to be the greatest of all shrubs, putting forth large branches and enabling the birds of the air to make nests in its shade.

This parable is relevant to our reframing in two ways. First, it tells us that we should celebrate paradox, not avoid or run from it. To avoid paradox is to shield ourselves from the kingdom of God. The mustard seed is a paradox, for the smallest of seeds becomes the largest of shrubs. Carl has astutely observed that Andy is faced with a paradox: the self-esteem he seeks through a career in acting may be undermined by that very career. Seeing this paradox, he seeks a way to protect Andy from it, to help him avoid it, or, at least, to cushion him against it. But our reframing does not counsel the avoidance of the paradox. Rather, it heightens it by encouraging Andy to consider an even wider array of possibilities in which the same paradox will be experienced. The reframing does not try to protect Andy's fragile self-esteem, but invites him to experience the paradox as fully as possible, as one might enter the eye of a storm. The reframing asks: What is gained—therapeutically, morally, and religiously—by advising Andy to avoid the basic paradox of his life (i.e., that the very domain in which he experiences self-esteem is also the domain that most undermines it)? To help Andy avoid this paradox is to invite him to walk away from life altogether.

Second, the parable is a testimony to the miracle of ordinary life. The parable is not about slow and steady growth from a little seed to a large shrub, but about the sharp juxtaposition of two radically different states of affairs. It is about the *smallest* of seeds and the *largest* of shrubs. This juxtaposition points not to normal expectations of growth but to a miracle. It is not about organic and biological development but about the gift-like nature of God's created order. The large shade from the small seed is a miracle, reflecting the surprising nature of the ordinary.[4] This is not utopianism, which envisions an ideal world that is precisely *out* of the ordinary, beyond the world of ordinary experience, but openness to the remarkable, unpredictable surprises of ordinary life.

Likewise, our reframing does not view Andy's situation from the perspective of what we might *normally* expect of Andy or of the world he intends to enter. If we viewed the matter in those terms, we would certainly agree that Andy should scale down his aspirations and try something less difficult. Acting *is* long and arduous, and there are few who succeed at it. But our reframing views the situation from the perspective of ordinary miracles. On the one hand, we have a rather inexperienced boy with low self-esteem. On the other, we have a boy who envisions himself as an accomplished, perhaps truly great actor. This is a sharp juxtaposition of two radically different states of affairs. But this same boy with low self-esteem might also envision himself as an effective diplomat, a very fine poet, a brilliant architect, a skillful psychologist, or a gifted manager. Our reframing does not try to reduce this radical juxtaposition between the boy and the vision of himself as a fine actor. Rather, it presses even further by encouraging a wider, more expansive vision.

So, where Andy's parents worry about his "exaggerated goals," the reframing, like the parable, makes a virtue of such exaggeration. The pastor who is attuned to Jesus' parabolic style is not uncomfortable with exaggeration. What would cause such a pastor discomfort is talk about being realistic, sensible, and practical. Andy does not need a pastor, of all persons, to tell him to be realistic. He does not need a pastor to tell him what a person in his situation can normally expect, what the "average expectable environment" affords.[5] What Andy needs from his pastor is the affirmation of ordinary miracles, the surprising gift-like nature of life itself. This is what the proposed reframing does. It affirms vision, it affirms miracle in life.

Once confronted with such affirmation, which is itself surprising, unexpected, and maybe disconcerting, there are at least three ways that Andy might respond. One, which we have already noted, is to see that his goal of becoming an actor is too visionary, too illusionary. He would begin to reconsider it, to entertain second thoughts about it, to see its potential pitfalls. This would not, in itself, violate the spirit of the parable, since his questions about an acting career would not have been forced upon him by fearful, cautionary adults. They would be based on a free choice, his own decision to be more realistic when confronted with the challenge to entertain even higher and more expansive visions. Carl might personally regret Andy's choice, even as Jesus was saddened when the rich ruler walked away from the vision set before him, or he might be inwardly pleased with Andy's decision because it would demonstrate his maturity. (Maturity, as John Weakland has defined it, is the ability to do something even though your parents have recommended it.)[6] More likely, Carl would view Andy's decision with a mixture of pleasure and regret—a common experience of pastors, and one reason why *ministry* is such a difficult profession.

Second, Andy might agree that his goal of becoming an actor is not visionary enough. Perhaps something even greater is in store for him, and he has been too narrowly focused on a single goal. Maybe it is not an acting career as such but something associated with it which is fueling his imagination. Maybe, as Carl suspects, acting is the one activity in Andy's life that has been a boost to his self-esteem. Because it is phrased positively, rather than negatively, the proposed reframing may enable Andy to recognize (in a nondefensive way) that his need for self-esteem is the driving force behind his desire to become an actor. This reframing would then invite him to consider what other avenues are available to him for gaining greater self-esteem. His willingness to consider other careers would be a clear indication that Carl's assessment is correct (i.e., that enhancement of self-esteem is a deep, underlying factor in Andy's desire to find a vocation which he can truly own).

A third possibility is that the reframing would reconfirm Andy's desire to become an actor. He might be convinced that acting is the greatest career he could possibly think of, that everything else pales in its light. If this were his reaction to the proposed reframing, an appropriate response from Carl would be, "Then you must do it. If acting means this much to you, you simply have to go through with it. You cannot let anyone talk you out of it." Along with this strong affirmation, Carl may also share with Andy his impression that Andy will be seeking self-esteem in a profession that is both prone to enhance and to undermine it. Better to raise Andy's consciousness about the paradox he confronts than to warn him that he is entering a difficult profession and will therefore need to work very hard. By being alerted to the paradox inherent in an acting career, Andy will be able to handle it better. People who are aware that the largest shrub comes from the smallest seed, and who want the largest shade possible, will not make the mistake of trading a handful of these seeds for one or two larger seeds of a different species. Furthermore, awareness of the paradox does not diminish one's sense of the miracle, but enhances it.

Finally, however, the important issue is not how Andy can be expected to respond to Carl's reframing, but that Carl is willing and able to reframe. Such reframing immediately removes Andy's decision from the context of *common sense,* of *normal expectations,* or of *average expectable outcomes,* and places it in the frame of *ordinary miracles.* Such reframing says that the miracle language of the gospels is neither dead nor extinct in our world today.

An indication that Andy understands the language of ordinary miracles is his comment that Jody stopped smoking *yesterday.* Viewed in terms of normal expectations and average expectable outcomes, we would have to say that it is much too early to tell whether Jody has quit smoking. One day of abstinence is not nearly enough evidence. But from the perspective of ordinary miracles, it is completely possible that, just yesterday, Jody's change in behavior became permanent and irrevocable. Andy clearly believes in ordinary miracles. He has an intuitive appreciation for the language of ordinary miracles and for its relevance to life today. To undermine this appreciation by insisting that only the language of common sense is acceptable and valid is to limit one's counsel to first-order change.

CONCLUSION

In presenting the cases of Laurie and Andy, I have deliberately chosen situations that are common to parish-centered pastoral care and counseling and have recommended reframings that are well within the usual range of parish pastors' competence and skill. I recognize that there are those, especially pastoral counseling specialists, who believe that the method of reframing is too difficult for the typical parish pastor. They contend that it should be employed only by specialists and only in formal counseling, not in the informal and occasional settings that are typical of parish ministry. But I believe that parish pastors, given their regular engagement with biblical texts in their preaching and teaching, have a special aptitude for the method of reframing. There are many psychotherapeutic procedures that *are* inappropriate for parish-centered pastoral care, but I do not accept the view that reframing is one of these (though I do acknowledge that there are certain reframing techniques that are beyond the typical parish pastor's competence and expertise). To be sure, the art of reframing requires imagination, wisdom, and the judicious exercise of authority. These capacities are not easily acquired, but neither are they the special gifts of a select group of professionals.

Some specialists argue that typical parish pastors should not employ the reframing method but should limit their care and counseling goals to first-order change. In their view, if second-order change is required, the parishioner should be referred to someone else (e.g., a pastoral counselor, psychotherapist, psychiatrist, marriage counselor, or social worker). Of course, there are many situations in which referral to another professional is appropriate, even mandated. But the indication that a second-order change is needed is not, in itself, grounds for referral. To limit parish pastors to interventions involving first-order change is to impose an unacceptable restriction on the Christian ministry itself. It is to exclude ministers of the gospel from involvement in the life-changing interventions to which the Bible itself attests. Since second-order change is fundamental to the Christian gospel, those who are called to serve this gospel cannot be precluded from involvement in situations that call for second-order change.[7]

The view that parish pastors should not be involved in second-order change efforts also reflects the common misconception that second-order change is always more difficult to achieve than first-order change. This is not necessarily true. Oftentimes, second-order changes come more easily precisely because they involve a radically new way of approaching the problem. When it occurs, second-order change seems to happen almost effortlessly. Sometimes, these changes seem too easy and simple, and so we mistrust them. Jesus made this very point through his healing ministry. After devoting months or years to expensive and painful procedures recommended by the medical practitioners of the day, the sick were amazed at how easily and quickly their symptoms disappeared when they expressed faith in Jesus. And yet many were suspicious and mistrustful because it happened too effortlessly. They predicted the change would not hold, that there would be a relapse, a backsliding. They also suspected Jesus of being a con-artist, a fake, a manipulator. But "reframes are not con-jobs. What makes a reframe work is that it adheres to the well-formedness conditions of a particular person's needs." Reframing requires the capacity to see another person's needs accurately, without distortion; this ability usually means being able to set our own needs aside, for the time being at least, and to suspend our usual tendency to view the other from the perspective of our own interests and aspirations. If we can do this, the rest is easy, as Jesus so clearly demonstrated.

PART 3

The Reframing
of Pastoral Care

CHAPTER SIX
The Inadequate Methods of Job's Counselors

In the two cases presented in chapters 4 and 5, my concern was to show how the reframing method works. We now examine the case of Job which enables us to compare the reframing method with other methods of pastoral care and counseling, and to demonstrate its superiority in certain instances.

To be sure, this case does not permit us to make a fair and unbiased test of the strengths and weaknesses of the other methods. Normally, in an unbiased test of competing counseling methods, proponents of the various methods are invited to counsel the same client before a public audience; then the client and the observers are asked for their assessments of the strengths and weaknesses of each approach. Whether these are fair tests of the counseling approaches is certainly open to question. But in any event, my purpose in using the Job case is not to pit these methods against one another, but to show that there are situations where the reframing method would clearly be the method of choice.

I also want to establish that, in such instances, the grounds for choosing the reframing method over other pastoral care and counseling methods are theological. For certain situations and certain individuals, the other methods are theologically deficient. Indeed, because the theological assumptions of Job's counselors are very explicit, this case, while ancient, is ideally suited for demonstrating that the theological assumptions behind the method are the critical issue. Also, because not one, but three counselors are involved, we can identify the theological deficiencies of three counseling methods which are commonly used by parish pastors. These are the methods of supportive counseling, crisis counseling, and counseling on ethical, value, and meaning issues. I suggest that Eliphaz is a supportive counselor, Bildad is a crisis counselor, and Zophar is a counselor on ethical, values, and meaning issues. We begin with the method of supportive counseling.

THE METHOD OF SUPPORTIVE
COUNSELING

In *Basic Types of Pastoral Care and Counseling,* Howard Clinebell distinguishes supportive from insight counseling. Insight methods aim at basic personality changes which they achieve by uncovering and dealing with previously hidden aspects of the personality. The goals of supportive counseling are more modest. Here, the pastor uses methods that stabilize, undergird, nurture, motivate, or guide troubled clients. Such methods enable these persons to handle their problems and relationships more constructively within whatever limits are imposed by their personality resources and circumstances. Thus, supportive counseling "does not employ uncovering methods and does not aim at depth insight or radical personality transformation. Instead, the goal is to help persons gain the strength and perspective to use their psychological and interpersonal resources (however limited) more effectively in coping creatively with their life situations."[1]

In actual practice, the distinction between insight and supportive counseling is usually a matter of emphasis and a choice of primary goals, rather than a rigid dichotomy. Some increased self-awareness and self-understanding may result from supportive counseling but, in general, supportive methods are more action-oriented and involve a larger degree of counselor activity and careful use of authority. In supportive counseling, the pastor makes more use of guidance, information, reassurance, inspiration, and planning. The pastor asks and answers more questions, and encourages or discourages certain forms of behavior.[2]

Clinebell lists seven procedures that may be used in supportive counseling:

1. Gratifying the dependency needs of the counselee by comforting, sustaining, inspiring, and guiding.

2. Enabling the counselee to experience emotional catharsis.
3. Helping the counselee to review the stress situation objectively, thus enabling him or her to make a wise decision.
4. Aiding the ego's defenses—the very opposite of uncovering, confronting, or probing.
5. Changing the life situation by helping the counselee to change his or her external circumstances.
6. Encouraging appropriate action by prescribing or recommending some activity that will keep the counselee functional.
7. Using religious resources (e.g., prayer, Bible, or devotional literature) which are intended to give counselees "fresh awareness that their lives have meaning transcending the pain and tragedy they face."[3]

Eliphaz, the first of Job's three counselors, has some clear affinities with the supportive counselor.

Eliphaz as Supportive Counselor

As the first to speak, Eliphaz senses his unenviable position. He speaks in a very cautious and yet sympathetic manner: "If one dares a word with you, can you handle it? But withhold a message—who could?" (4:2). He continues on a positive note, pointing out that Job had strengthened many others through words of personal encouragement and guidance, and asking Job whether the words of assurance he had offered to others when *they* were troubled were not also applicable to *him?* "Is not the fear of God your confidence, and your hope the very integrity of your ways?" (4:6).

Next, he assures Job that he can take great comfort in his innocence, because God sustains the innocent and the upright, and does not cut them off. After relating a personal experience in which he felt very vulnerable and afraid himself, Eliphaz appeals to Job to call on God because there is simply no one else to whom he might turn: "As for me, I would seek God and commit my case to God, who does great inscrutable deeds, wonders beyond reckoning" (5:8). God exalts the lowly, lifts the forlorn to safety, and saves the simple and needy from destruction: "So the poor have hope" (5:10-16).

In encouraging Job to commit his case to God, Eliphaz clearly regards Job as innocent. He does not suggest or imply that Job's difficulties are the result of his own wrongdoing. What happened to Job was, in all likelihood, just part of human life. Individuals suffer for no particular reason. Yet, the fact that Job still lives, and survived the calamity, is reason to be hopeful. On the other hand, he also notes that Job's sufferings might be viewed as God's corrective discipline, as a warning (5:17). This is a benevolent warning, a sign that Job is among the blessed. Sufferings in this case do not lead to death, but to restoration: "He it is who inflicts pain and then binds; he wounds, but his hands then heal" (5:18). Here, Eliphaz intimates that God may have caused or permitted some of Job's difficulties, not, however, because he was guilty or deserving of punishment, but as a benevolent warning.

The important point for Eliphaz, however, is that while Job has experienced calamity, this is not the final word, for everything will be set right again: "You will know that your tent is at peace; when you visit your fold, nothing will be missing" (5:24). In fact, he assures Job that his future life will actually be better than it was before the calamity: "You will know your progeny is great: Your offspring will be as the grass of the earth. You will reach the grave full of vigor, like a sheaf of grain in season" (5:25-26).

The approach that Eliphaz takes with Job has clear affinities with supportive counseling. Note his use of the seven procedures set forth by Clinebell:

1. Gratifying dependency needs of the counselee. An older man than Job, Eliphaz addresses him in a kind, noncondescending way. He questions the wisdom of speaking to Job when he is so obviously in pain. But he recalls that Job sustained others in similar circumstances. He does not exploit Job's dependency, and he certainly does not treat him like a child. He establishes a supportive atmosphere which communicates the desire to sustain, inspire, and guide Job as needed.

2. Enabling emotional catharsis. Some catharsis had occurred before any of the counselors spoke. Much of it comes later as the dialogues continue. Does Eliphaz encourage such catharsis? Emphatically yes. His refusal to accuse Job of wrongdoing and his assurance that Job is the victim of forces beyond his control gives Job license to lament his situation, and to continue to plead his innocence. Also, Eliphaz's reference to his own experience of vulnerability and fear gives Job encouragement to talk about his anxiety and his fears about what has been happening to him.

3. Objective review of the situation. Eliphaz advises Job to consider that while he has lost so very much, he himself is still here. This may seem like small consolation to a man who has suffered such loss, but it is an objective fact that Job would do well to remember in reviewing his situation. Another point that Eliphaz makes is that Job is innocent of wrongdoing and may take comfort in this knowledge. Would God abandon a man who is so clearly innocent? If he has survived the calamities that happen to the good and wicked alike, can he not now assume that God will bring him healing and deliverance? With this objective review of the situation, Eliphaz advises Job to call upon God for help. This is the wise thing to do; not only because God alone can help him, but more important, because God is prepared to help him, and already waiting for him to ask.

4. Aiding the ego's defenses. Eliphaz does not challenge Job's perception of himself as a righteous man. On the contrary, he affirms this self-understanding, and uses it as the basis of his advice to Job. In building up Job's ego-defenses in this way, Eliphaz is not engaging in deceit or flattery. It is clear to him, as it is to us, that Job is a person of very great character. Even his suggestion that Job's suffering may have a disciplinary purpose is an appeal to his ego integrity. It suggests that this could be the only reason that God would afflict Job, and that God is confident Job is a person who will be able to learn from these sufferings and emerge stronger than ever.

5. Changing the life situation. Eliphaz realizes that he cannot effect a direct or immediate change in Job's external circumstances. In this regard, he is like the modern parish pastor who cannot provide medical or substantial financial assistance, but can have a profound effect on the counselee's attitude. Thus, Eliphaz's goal is to help Job adjust, mainly through a change in his attitude toward his condition. He proposes that Job turn to God for help, doing so in the confidence that God would never abandon him and is already disposed to help him. He anticipates that this change in Job's attitude will effect changes in his external circumstances, but he never suggests or implies that God's help is conditional on Job's seeking assistance. Instead, he is convinced that God must help Job because it is God's nature to do so. God inflicts pain and then binds. God wounds and then heals. Because the one has happened to him, Job can expect the other.[4] Thus, the change Eliphaz seeks— his counseling goal—is to help Job recover his earlier confidence in God.

6. Encouraging appropriate action. In one sense, Eliphaz fails to encourage appropriate action because he does not prescribe a practical, everyday activity, which is what Clinebell has in mind:

> When persons are stunned or paralyzed by feelings of anxiety, defeat, failure, damaged self-esteem, or tragic loss, it is often helpful for the pastor to prescribe some activity that will keep them functioning and in touch with people. This diminishes the tendency to retreat into depression and to withdraw from relationships. Constructive activity gives temporary structure to the person's chaotic world as well as providing ways of changing the painful situation.[5]

Eliphaz does not recommend any such concrete activity, but he advises Job to take constructive action by calling on God and committing his case to God. He evidently assumes that Job knows what concrete actions would be called for were he to call upon God (presumably, some form of prayer or supplication).

7. Using religious resources. Eliphaz certainly uses religious resources to give Job "fresh awareness" that his life has meaning, transcending the pain and tragedy he is experiencing. He does not use written documents comparable to the Bible or devotional literature, nor does he actually engage Job in verbal or silent prayer. But certainly the tone of his counseling is religious in that it uses theological concepts and language derived from the religious tradition that he represents. In fact, his whole approach to his counseling of Job is so deeply rooted in this tradition that it stands as a critique of our modern tendency to identify religious resources as such, as though they are add-ons to the counseling process, and not essential aspects of it. With Eliphaz, there is no such distinction between religious resources and the counseling process itself.

Did supportive counseling work with Job? No, it did not. It only increased Job's anger which, in turn, caused Eliphaz to abandon his supportive tone and to become much more accusatory in subsequent conversations with Job. Job was especially incensed by Eliphaz's view that what had happened to Job was just a part of life. Job was convinced that God was to blame for his sufferings. They were the work of God, the cruel and vicious *Hunter*: "For the arrows of God are in me, my spirit imbibes their poison" (6:4). A cruel Hunter, God is also a *Seeing Eye,* a watcher of humans who takes sadistic pleasure in observing the physical and moral disintegration of humans (7:20). God could simply pardon transgressions. But, no, God insists on their exposure, taking perverse pleasure in the shame and humiliation of mortals. So why should Job seek after God, as Eliphaz suggests, when God is searching for him for the purpose of humiliating him?

For Job, then, the fundamental flaw in Eliphaz, as well as the other colleagues, is that they fail to see this dark and threatening side of God. They see God only as trustworthy. Other friends have avoided and rejected Job through physical distance. These three friends avoid and reject him psychologically, by viewing his tragedy through God-trusting eyes. He challenges his friends: Abandon your trust in God, and you will see my tragedy for what it is, and you will see God as you have never allowed yourselves to see God before, as the enemy—Hunter, Seeing Eye—who terrifies his victim (6:4). They may perceive Job as the victim of a calamity which strikes the innocent and wicked alike. They can rationalize his sufferings as being part of the "human condition." They can even, in their bolder moments, suggest that God has visited these sufferings on Job as a benevolent warning to a righteous man against complacency. But Job sees it very differently: He is the prey of God, the relentlessly vicious Hunter who attacks with poison arrows, and the Seeing Eye who takes perverse delight in Job's exposure and humiliation. Why won't Eliphaz and his friends see this? Because they are *afraid* of its implications. If they agree with Job that God is his adversary, what will remain of their own confidence in God? And, if they agree with him, how can they be sure that God will not attack them for their agreement with Job?

The Theology of Supportive Counseling

Eliphaz began as a supportive counselor but then abandoned this approach, obviously sensing that his original method had not worked. Why did it fail? I say its failure was due to the theology that undergirds the method of supportive counseling. Supportive pastoral care and counseling affirms—indeed must affirm—the trustworthiness of God. Everything Eliphaz said in the first round of dialogues was rooted in his confidence that God would look kindly on Job if he would turn to God. God could be trusted. But, as far as Job was concerned, this advice meant that Eliphaz could not fully and truly empathize with a friend, like Job, who had lost his trust in God. Eliphaz could not see God as Job saw God, however much he tried to empathize with Job and his perspective.

Job accused Bildad and Zophar, Eliphaz's colleagues, of the same partiality toward God. This, however, is an especially serious issue for the supportive counselor, because the ability to comfort, sustain, inspire, and guide depends on the counselee's perception that the counselor can be relied upon. As Clinebell puts it, "In supportive care and counseling the relationship *per se* is the primary instrument of change. Maintaining a dependable, nurturing relationship is the heart of the process. By relating trustfully to the pastor, such persons are able to draw on the pastor's inner strength."[6] But, if the counselee believes that the counselor is actually allied with his adversary, as Job does, how can the counselor be perceived as trustworthy, as a source of inner strength? It is difficult enough in cases where the counselor is suspected of favoring another counselee (as in marriage counseling). But the problem is even greater when the counselor is perceived to have a deep personal investment in maintaining a positive relationship with the counselee's most powerful enemy. This is the dilemma that the supportive pastoral counselor faces when attempting to counsel a person who views God as a mortal threat.

Job did not trust Eliphaz to be impartial, so he rejected his efforts to guide, to reassure, and to inspire him. Job felt that Eliphaz's efforts in his behalf were actually motivated by a desire to defend God. He was not at all persuaded that Eliphaz's primary concern was for him; instead, he felt that Eliphaz's efforts only served his own theological viewpoint, which he continued to affirm in the face of Job's challenges against it.

Some would argue, of course, that this link between the method of supportive counseling and the belief in a trustworthy God is a problem only in cases where the counselee no longer looks to God as a source of hope. Since most persons with whom pastors counsel view God as trustworthy, this leaves the supportive method intact. But is this really so? Is the attitude of Job toward God so unusual or exceptional? Isn't his loss of trust in God much more common, and therefore a much more serious threat to supportive counseling, than this argument supposes?

In a study of parents who had suffered the loss of a daughter or son to cancer or a blood disorder, Judith A. Cook and Dale W. Wimberley found that the three most common responses of parents to the child's death were (1) to blame God or question the mercy of God; (2) to view the death as a punishment for the parent's own wrongdoing; and (3) to see the death as intended by God to serve a good and useful purpose.[7] The authors note that the first response was given by parents who had expected God to heal their child, and were bitterly disappointed when the child died. Thus, blaming God was most likely among parents who were especially confident that God would help them in their time of desperate need. Therefore, the persons who were among the most trusting of God lost confidence in God. Job's case is neither rare nor unusual. We dare not ignore the challenge which Job poses for supportive counseling on the dubious claim that his situation is uncommon.

Some would retort that Job's view of God is simply wrong, that God is not, in fact, a God who is vindictive and cruel. Certainly, most of us would agree that Job has an unduly negative view of God. But conversely, perhaps the theology which undergirds supportive counseling reflects an unduly positive, even romanticized view of God. Through his sufferings, Job has experienced the darker side of God, and has come to see God as a more complex being than he had previously understood God to be.

Gordon W. Allport has said that a complex or differentiated sentiment is more mature than a non-differentiated one because it takes more of reality into account. He illustrates this point with two students' descriptions of their fathers. One student wrote: "Dad is a perfect father. He loves his family and his family loves him. He is looked up to in all the town, highly admired. He will help anyone. He is noted for his fairness and honesty. Fairness and honesty are Dad." Allport says that this description betrays an undifferentiated sentiment: "The father is just perfect; everything about him is right. The student's devotion to him is marked by such abandon that we suspect she has never made a close and analytic inspection of his character, and even that her lavish praise may cover some repressed animosity." The other student wrote of her father: "He is somewhat unsocial, but dramatic enough to be pleasing in company; irritable, but not at all ill-natured; conscientious, hardworking, puritanical; timid in some things, dogged in others. His imagination is shown in his love of travel, but is not much in evidence otherwise." Allport observes: "This daughter likewise approves of her father. Yet, unlike the first, she is observant, critical, not merely abandoned in her admiration. One suspects that the very *differentiation* of the sentiment in the second case prevents repressed criticisms and hostility from forming. Her view of her father, if more complex, is more realistic."[8]

Job's sufferings and losses have led him to view God in a much more differentiated way than he did before his calamities. He is now able to recognize the terrible side of God, describing God as a Hunter and a Seeing Eye. These new recognitions, so recently achieved, have virtually obliterated his strongly positive picture of God. Thus, Eliphaz's efforts to comfort him with the trustworthiness of God are deeply and profoundly offensive to him. To Job, there is more to God—much more—than Eliphaz is prepared to see and to acknowledge.

In the normal course of life, we are probably comfortable with Eliphaz's theology, with its emphasis on God's trustworthiness. But when we see this theology at work, informing the counseling of a man whose life has come crashing down, we surely sympathize with Job and his more complex and questioning view of God. The disputation between Eliphaz and Job no doubt reflects the theological arguments that we have within ourselves. At times, we are attracted to the views of Eliphaz, and agree with the assurances that his theology offers. At other times, however, we are drawn to the darker view that Job expresses; in these moments, we sense that Job has seen more deeply into the mystery of God. Perhaps the difference between Eliphaz and Job is the difference between what William James has called "healthy-minded" and "sick-minded" religion. For James, sick-minded religion, as reflected by Job, is the more complex and ultimately deeper form of religion because it does not flinch from the reality of evil.[9]

Supportive counseling is necessarily healthy-minded. Eliphaz's assurance to Job that he can turn to God is the very foundation of supportive counseling. But the concluding words of Job's response to Eliphaz attest to a very different experience of God: "God has made my heart sink. God has filled me with dread. For I am indeed cut off, my darkness and ominous gloom veils my face" (23:16-17). The supportive counselor can certainly "accept" words of this kind from a counselee ("I know how you feel") and may even confess to having "felt that way myself" (witness Eliphaz's account of his own experience of helpless fear). But may a supportive counselor, as counselor, actually believe and operate on the belief that Job has spoken truly about God? No. In supportive counseling, the counselee needs to be able to draw on the counselor's inner strength—the counselor's conviction that God is not the counselee's problem but the ultimate solution. When functioning in the role of supportive counselor, we simply cannot believe, or even imagine, that God is the God of Job's experience, the *Seeing Eye* who delights in Job's humiliation and the *Hunter* who has poisoned Job and left him for dead.

According to Clinebell, supportive counseling is like an orthopedic device that has two valid uses: as a splint to provide temporary support while a broken bone heals, and as a brace to allow a permanently crippled person to function. These orthopedic images indicate that the goals of supportive counseling are quite modest. Perhaps we should not be critical of it for its limited, if not simplistic theology. Yet, supportive counseling is especially recommended for persons who find themselves in situations as painful, agonizing, and intractable as Job's. Its goals are modest precisely because the sufferings it confronts are so painful and deep. Its primary goal, according to Clinebell, "is to help persons continue to function at their own optimal level, however limited, in spite of their difficult and unchangeable life situations."[10] Persons in such difficult situations may not always be as outspoken as Job in voicing their loss of hope in God, as vivid in their portrayal of what it is like to be God's enemy, or as open about their desire for the relief of death. But these words, perceptions, and desires are never far from the surface with those whose suffering is deep and painful. Also close to the surface is their feeling that a pastor, no matter how personally supportive and sympathetic, cannot truly accept these words, perceptions, and desires. Our analysis of supportive counseling via the case of Job indicates that this feeling is well-founded. It is not merely a reflection of a desperate counselee's diminished physical and mental capacities.

THE METHOD OF CRISIS COUNSELING

We turn, next, to Bildad and the method of crisis counseling. Because pastors are frequently called upon to minister to persons who are experiencing a crisis, this method is among the most discussed and recommended in the pastoral care field. Clinebell suggests that a pastor's assistance to persons in crisis has four aspects: (1) the general ministry of care; (2) informal crisis counseling; (3) short-term formal crisis counseling (i.e., one to five sessions); and (4) long-term counseling therapy to help persons repair the psychological causes and/or consequences of severe crisis.[11] He notes that everyone "needs increased care and nurture when [he or she is] going through deep water," but "only a small percentage need formal counseling, and even a smaller percentage need reparative counseling." So, he focuses on short-term and informal crisis counseling (or what is often called "crisis intervention").

Because crisis intervention is the most relevant to the case of Job, our assessment of crisis counseling is limited to it. Crisis intervention is employed in crisis situations which are not amenable even to short-term counseling. A popular crisis intervention approach is the ABC model developed by Warren Jones. It involves three steps: (1) Achieving contact with the person in crisis; (2) Boiling the problem down to its essentials; and (3) Coping actively with the problem. In his book, *Crisis Counseling,* Howard W. Stone points out that achieving contact involves the use of *attending behaviors* (e.g., offering a cup of coffee) and *listening* for the presenting problem and the precipitation of the crisis. Boiling the problem down to its essentials involves *responding,* especially to the meaning of the crisis for the person who is experiencing it; and *focusing,* by centering on the present situation and source of stress, and filtering out irrelevant data. Coping actively with the problem involves five procedures: establishing goals, taking inventory of resources, formulating alternatives, taking action, and reviewing the action and refining the goals.[12]

Because the third step—coping actively—includes so much, Clinebell has recently revised the Jones ABC model to include four steps. It is now the ABCD crisis intervention model. The first two steps remain the same, but the third has been revised: (3) Challenging the individual to take constructive action on some part of the problem. The new fourth step is (4) Developing an ongoing growth-action plan.[13]

David K. Switzer is also an advocate of the Jones method, but proposes his own CFC model: (1) *Contact:* Achieve contact with the client by establishing the relationship, identifying the presenting problem and the precipitating events, assisting catharsis, and building hopeful expectations; (2) *Focus:* Focus on the present situation by exploring the situation and identifying the threat; and (3) *Cope:* Help the client cope through an inventory of problem-solving resources, assisting in decision making, emphasizing relationships with others, and summarizing new learning.[14] Stone concludes his discussion of the ABCD method by emphasizing the vital importance of follow-up. We might therefore integrate these various models into a C-F-C-F method, which would include Switzer's Contact-Focus-Cope and Stone's Follow-up.

But what we name the steps is not the critical issue. What matters is that crisis intervention involves helping a person identify a problem, focus on viable alternatives, take action, and evaluate the action that is taken. Crisis intervention theory emphasizes the need to make a decision and carry it out, even if this decision deals with only a small part of the crisis area and does not resolve the problem as a whole. As Clinebell puts it, the human personality is like a muscle: "Using it in constructive thinking and action tends to strengthen its coping abilities."[15] The goal of crisis intervention is to get the person to abandon what Switzer calls the "do-nothing inertia" which crises inevitably create, even in individuals who are ordinarily decisive and action-oriented persons.

Job is an excellent candidate for crisis intervention counseling. Not only has he been immobilized by his losses; he also illustrates the "cumulative effect" of crisis. As Clinebell explains: "The particular crisis or loss that motivates a person to seek pastoral help often is only the last straw, the most recent in a series of stressful changes and losses. Such a series, within a limited time period, has a cumulative effect in which one plus one produces more than two units of stress in the person."[16] Clinebell cites the Stress Scale of Common Life Experiences developed by Thomas H. Holmes and R. H. Rahe, professors in psychiatry at the University of Washington. These psychiatrists assigned the death of one's spouse a stress score of 100, and then listed 42 additional life events, ranging from a mean stress value of 73 (for divorce) to 11 (for minor violations of the law).

Job's life events, their rankings, and mean stress values (MSV), include the following:

- Death of a close family member, tied for 4th, msv = 63
- Major personal injury or illness, 6th, msv = 53
- Major change in financial state, 16th, msv = 38
- Major change in number of arguments with spouse, 19th, msv = 35
- Major change in living conditions, 28th, msv = 25

How we should calculate the deaths of all six children is difficult to determine. If we take the conservative approach and assign the stress value of only one death, Job's cumulative stress score is at least 214 points, more than double the stress that accompanies the major cause of stress—the death of one's spouse—or the equivalent of three divorces. If we count all the children's deaths, his stress score is 479, nearly five times the amount of stress that results from a spouse's death. If we view his strained relations with his wife as akin to marital separation, the third most severe life event, his score, on the most conservative basis, would be 289 and, on the more liberal but probably more realistic basis, 544.

Holmes and Rahe found that among individuals with a cumulative stress score in one year of between 150 and 299, approximately 50 percent became sick, either physically, psychologically, or psychosomatically. Some 80 percent of those with stress levels over 300 became sick. Clinebell concludes that this stress rating scale "can alert pastoral counselors and lay crises carers to the importance of searching for clusters of life changes from which people are suffering cumulative stress overloads."[17] He also notes that some major life stresses are not included in this scale, including spouse and child abuse, rape, the loss of faith and values, poverty, and the fear of nuclear holocaust. In Job's case, we could add such stresses as the loss of friends, loss of respect in the family and community, loss of self-respect, and physical disfigurement. Even if we agree with Switzer that "the crisis is within the person and not inherently within the event itself," and that individuals react very differently to these life events,[18] there is no question that Job was a prime candidate for "cumulative stress overload."

Switzer also notes that objectively *positive* events are sometimes experienced as highly stressful. The Holmes and Rahe scale supports this claim. Getting married, for example, is ranked seventh, with a mean stress value of 50. Marital reconciliation is ranked ninth, with a mean stress value of 45. On the Holmes and Rahe scale, Job's restoration at the end of the story (42:10-17) is nearly as stressful as his losses. It included marital reconciliation (msv = 50), gaining a new family member (msv = 39), major change in financial state (msv = 38), major change in living conditions (msv = 25), and major change in eating habits (msv = 15). The total is 167 stress points, based on the conservative approach of assigning the stress value of only one new family member gained, or 362 stress points, based on the more liberal and realistic accounting of six new family members. On the other hand, while Job's stress level as a consequence of his restoration is nearly as high as in the time of his losses, the stress levels of *individual* life events were much higher during the calamitous time, and thus, when viewed individually, were significantly more stressful.

Bildad as Crisis Counselor

Bildad begins in the traditional disputational style, describing Job's response to Eliphaz as a "big wind." But then he settles down to the task at hand by asking a very pointed question: "Does God pervert justice? Does God pervert the right?" (8:3). Without waiting for Job to reply, since his question was obviously rhetorical, Bildad offers an explanation for the tragedy that had befallen Job: "Your children must have sinned against him, and he dispatched them over to their wickedness" (8:4). Thus, all that has happened can be explained by the fact that Job's children did something to incite God's anger.

From this explanation, Bildad moves quite swiftly to consider what Job might do about the whole matter. Of course, his children are beyond saving. But Job's own situation is not hopeless: "But you, if you go early to God, and implore the mercy of God, if you are pure and upright, then he will rouse himself for you and restore your righteous abode" (8:5-6). Many commentators believe that Bildad is advising Job here to make a ritual sacrifice for his children's sins. Once he has done this, God will respond favorably, and restore Job's health and livelihood. If Job takes this rather simple course of action, the results will be most impressive: "If your beginning was small, your end will flourish indeed" (8:7).

But why should Job do this? Why should he go to God, confident that God will restore his life? Bildad answers with a parable about two plants (8:12, 16-19):

> One plant is still fresh and uncut when it withers, quicker than grass. Another plant stays fresh, even in the sun. Its shoots reach beyond its garden. Over a rock pile its roots wind; a house of stone it spies. If its place should swallow it and deny, saying, "I did not see you," such is the joy of its way that from the dust it shoots up elsewhere.

What is the meaning of this parable? Bildad explains: Those who forget God are like the first plant. For them, there is no hope (8:13). But those who remain blameless, who continue to trust in God, are like the second shoot. They do not escape adversity, but they possess the inner strength to "shoot up elsewhere" when the place they inhabit is no longer hospitable: "The rocky ground which devours the plant may deny it ever saw the extended tendrils or roots, but the plant rejoices in the new life that rises from the dust."[19] Thus, in death there is new life, and in destruction there are already the signs of renewal. Out of dust and ashes, new life is coming forth, and the same renewal is possible for those who trust in God. In effect, Job is like a plant that had the misfortune of putting down roots in an inhospitable environment. But Bildad anticipates for Job a new beginning, a revival and vindication. Even now, his life is beginning to rise again.

The approach that Bildad takes with Job has some clear affinities with crisis intervention counseling. The first step of crisis intervention is achieving contact which, in Switzer's view, involves establishing the relationship, identifying the presenting problem and precipitating events, assisting catharsis, and building hopeful expectations. Bildad does this. He sits quietly for a week before speaking to Job. This enables him not only to establish the relationship but also to identify Job's presenting problem and the events (i.e., the many losses) that precipitated it. This week of silence also assists emotional catharsis, as Job's lament in chapter 3 so clearly demonstrates. Then, as he begins to speak, Bildad attempts to build hopeful expectations, assuring Job that he does not believe Job himself is guilty of wrongdoing and has not brought any of this upon himself. Thus, Bildad succeeds in making contact.

The second step in crisis intervention is focus. For Stone, this involves centering on the present situation and source of stress, and filtering out irrelevant data. For Switzer, it means exploring the present situation and identifying the source of the threat. Bildad encourages such focusing. He asks whether God perverts justice, and certain that the answer is no, he begins to look for other explanations for Job's difficulties. He is equally certain that Job is a blameless man, that he has done nothing personally to bring all this tragedy upon himself. Therefore, the crisis must have been precipitated by something else. The explanation might have been one of the various factors that Eliphaz enumerated—for example, that tragedy happens to the righteous and unrighteous alike or that Job was the subject of God's benevolent discipline. But Bildad tries to focus on what is clearly known or knowable about the situation and to leave these more speculative ideas to others. It seems clear to him that Job's children were involved in sinful behavior that was offensive to God, and that God's justice demanded that they be punished for it.

The grounds for Bildad's assignment of blame to Job's children are rather circumstantial and certainly not conclusive. Bildad may have based his suggestion on his observation that Job had been making ritual offerings to God because "it may be that my sons have sinned, and cursed God in their hearts" (1:5). But the important issue is not whether Bildad's reasoning is correct, but that he has made an effort to *focus* the problem, to boil it down to its essentials. If God is directly angry with Job, that would be one issue. But if God's anger is directed toward his children, this is a very different matter. Job's view of his current situation, and what he decides to do about it, will be radically different depending on which of these two explanations he accepts. For Bildad, the basic problem is that Job's sons angered God; while Job is presently suffering the consequences of his sons' actions, these sufferings, because they have nothing to do with Job's own behavior, are temporary.

The third step in crisis intervention involves helping the counselee cope. For Switzer, this means taking an inventory of problem-solving resources, assisting in decision making, emphasizing relationships with others, and summarizing what has been learned from the actions taken. For Stone, it means establishing goals, taking an inventory of resources for achieving these goals, formulating the available alternatives, taking action, and making a review of the action taken, which will lead to refinement of the goals.

Bildad moves into this stage by encouraging Job to take actions that are clearly within his power. What Job should do is go to God the very next morning and implore God's mercy for what his sons have done. By doing this, he will begin a process that will result in the recovery of his health and livelihood. This proposal is consistent with the expectation that the crisis counselor will help the counselee to decide on the next step and then take it. Bildad's confidence that this step will have positive results also reflects the crisis counselor's view that taking even small steps begins to improve the counselee's self-confidence, hope, and sense of competence, enabling him or her to take progressively larger steps.

Bildad's proposed course of action is also based on an informal inventory of Job's resources, especially his assessment of Job's inner strength. Crisis intervention theory emphasizes the counselee's coping capacities as his or her major resource. Bildad's parable of the two plants speaks to his belief that Job has the inner strength needed for coping effectively with the situation. By reinforcing his proposal with the parable, Bildad communicates his belief that Job will be able to make a new life for himself once he takes the step of imploring God's mercy for his children's actions. For Bildad, as for crisis counselors, the goal is to get Job to decide to do something. In a crisis like this, even a person who is accustomed to acting decisively, as Job certainly was, is in danger of becoming immobilized. Bildad sees this, and begs Job to return to his custom of going to God in the morning and imploring God's mercy. If Job could do this before calamity struck, he still has the inner resources to do it now.

The fourth stage of crisis intervention is the follow-up. This does not occur in Job's case because Job refuses to act on Bildad's recommendation. Instead, their conversation focuses on their disagreements concerning the issues normally addressed and agreed upon in the coping stage. Job disagrees with Bildad's assessments of available problem-solving resources and on the appropriate action to take. Since no action was taken, there could be no review, and no summary of what had been learned from this action. Clearly, Bildad's efforts at crisis intervention had failed. As failure became apparent, he, like Eliphaz, became more hostile toward Job, accusing him directly of wrongdoing.

Why had Bildad's efforts failed? Close study of Job's response to Bildad indicates that these efforts did not succeed because Bildad did not take account of the inner change that Job had undergone as a direct result of the crisis itself. This change was in Job's perception of himself as a righteous man. Bildad's proposed course of action was based on the assumption that Job was guiltless, not morally responsible for what had happened to him. Job did not challenge the objective truth of this assumption, but he told Bildad that he no longer *felt* righteous. This change in Job's feelings about himself is poignantly expressed in the following exclamation: "Though I am innocent, my mouth would condemn me; though I am blameless, he would declare me perverse. I am blameless! I do not know myself! I loath my life!" (9:20-21). This juxtaposition of "I am blameless" and "I do not know myself" is an acknowledgement that Job does not recognize his former self.[20] He does not doubt his innocence, but no longer is his righteousness a powerful motivating force in his life, for the more he asserts his claim to innocence, the more he appears to be guilty. He no longer derives any personal satisfaction or strength from his plea of innocence, his claim to righteousness.

In this acknowledgment, Job expresses the terrible tragedy of innocent suffering. To those who would argue that he is able to stand on the fact of his innocence, Job claims that the suffering he has been made to endure changes everything. There is no satisfaction to be gained from being an innocent victim, for his victimization undermines his felt sense of innocence. Objectively, he knows he has done nothing wrong. But the experience he has been enduring has called his innocence into question, creating self-doubts that would never have been entertained had he not been put into the position of a victim. Even if God acknowledged his innocence, would this restore his own inner spirit? Would it restore his love for life? For Job, the victim, the answer is no.

How then could he possibly respond affirmatively to Bildad's advice and recommendations? Is it a simple matter of the plant leaving its inhospitable environment and relocating in another? What about the permanent wounds that the plant carries with it, the awareness that it came close to death? And what about the plant's knowledge that the soil engaged in treachery and deception, pretending not to know that the plant was even there? Will the plant ever be able to trust again? As a result of his victimization, Job has suffered the "spoiling" of his identity as a righteous man.[21] He can still claim this identity on objective grounds, but subjectively, it is all but ruined for him, permanently besmirched: "If I am guilty, woe is me. But if I am innocent—I cannot lift my head, I am so sated with shame and so saturated with misery" (10:15).

The Theology of Crisis Counseling

From the viewpoint of contemporary crisis intervention theory, Bildad's counseling technique can certainly be faulted. He was overly confident that he had correctly identified the root of Job's problems (i.e., the sins of his children). While crisis counselors are often expected to be forceful and even confrontational because it is important that they succeed in shifting the counselee out of his "do-nothing inertia," Bildad was unusually dogmatic and highly confrontational.

On the other hand, the basic problem here is not that Bildad was poorly skilled in matters of procedure and technique. The deeper issue was that he ignored Job's testimony to the change in his self-image, caused by his victimization. Objectively, Job continued to view himself as blameless, but he took no comfort in this knowledge because he no longer *felt* blameless. This is a very common experience of innocent victims of violence (e.g., victims of rape, incest, and child abuse); it is also common among victims of natural and economic disasters, war, and epidemics. They *know* they are personally innocent of wrongdoing, and yet the crisis robs them of their *sense* of innocence. They feel ashamed and humiliated. They experience themselves as failures, their identities permanently damaged. This was Job's condition. He complained to Bildad that he no longer experienced himself as a blameless man. For a person whose very identity was based on his righteousness, this was a very powerful confession and reflected a profound negative transformation.

Yet, Bildad's counseling efforts were based on the assumption that Job's sense of self was unchanged, in spite of the crisis he was going through. It never occurred to him to question whether Job still had the inner resources he needed to cope with the crisis. He merely assumed that these resources were there and could be activated now for Job's restoration and rehabilitation.

Job resented this assumption. He reminded Bildad that his inner resources had been based on his positive self-perception, on his view of himself as a man of high integrity and unquestioned personal honor. Since he no longer felt that way about himself, he was bereft of inner resources.

In my reading of crisis intervention literature, I have found that Bildad's error is not untypical. While concern for the counselee's damaged self-perception is often found in longer-term crisis counseling, it is generally missing in discussions of informal crisis intervention. In the concern to move the counselee to action, however small and insignificant this action may be, crisis intervention gives no systematic attention to the effects of the crisis on the counselee's self-image. This is not to say that persons engaged in informal crisis intervention are insensitive to this issue, but only that the method developed by Jones and refined by others includes no systematic attention to it. This method assumes that getting counselees to act is largely a matter of exploring alternative courses of action, making an inventory of the counselee's problem-solving resources, and achieving a good fit between the course of action chosen and the problem-solving resources available. But Job is saying that the situation is more complex than this. He no longer experiences himself as a righteous man, so he cannot take any actions based on the assumption of his righteousness. Subjectively, to do so would be false and hypocritical. On the other hand, it would be just as false and hypocritical to take actions that assume his *un*righteousness, because he knows that this is not his objective situation. So Job concludes that he can take no action at all. His situation is a classic double bind. It is not surprising that he adopts a do-nothing inertia. Practically speaking, he has no other choice. Crisis intervention theory assumes the existence of a number of options or alternative courses of action. But Job's crisis experience is precisely the crisis of discovering that he *has no options.*

This discovery, however, has one positive effect that Bildad, as crisis interventionist, totally ignores. Job's awareness that he can take no action in the real world activates his imagination. The image that comes to mind as he responds to Bildad is one of a redeemer whom he envisions "rising on the dust." This image, in turn, produces an imaginary scenario of the redeemer avenging Job's integrity in the heavenly assemblies (19:25-27). So, Job, knowing that he cannot act for himself, imagines a redeemer who will rise and speak for him. As the scenario of vindication in the heavenly assembly enters his mind, he has a sense of what it means to *feel* righteous again. No doubt, this feeling passes as quickly as it arises, but a little spark of hope has been ignited in him. If he were to consider taking action, it would be based on this new and largely unfamiliar inner resource, not on the inner resources which were developed before the crisis occurred. Yet, throughout his conversation with Bildad, Job remains adamant that he is out of options.

Thus, the dialogue between Bildad and Job points to the effects of the crisis itself on the self-perceptions of the sufferer. For Job, these effects are all-important; for Bildad, they are of small significance. Switzer indirectly alludes to this difficulty when he emphasizes that "the crisis is within the person and not inherently within the event itself"; but in developing this point, he focuses on the sufferer's "self-appraisal in terms of capacity to cope effectively with this degree of threat."[22] Self-perception is therefore understood mainly as the counselee's appraisal of his coping capacities and not as the counselee's inner sense of self, as reflected in the dramatic shift in Job's subjective sense of identity from blameless man to hapless victim.

This radical change in self-perception is fundamentally a theological matter. While some people would view it as a psychological issue having no obvious theological implications or meaning, the case of Job enables us to see that a radical change in self-perception has deep religious significance, whether the counselee is aware of this or not. It is religious because, as Job sees so clearly, a radical change in self-perception necessarily alters one's perception and experience of God. We are not independent selves. We are selves by virtue of our relation to other selves. Who is God but a self who is everlasting, who is impossible to escape or ignore? Therefore, as Job's self-perception was radically altered, his perception of God was also dramatically changed. His loss of confidence in himself and in God, leading him to place tentative hopes in another agent—a redeemer who would avenge him *against* God—were two sides of the same coin. Thus, the failure of crisis intervention to register Job's change in self-perception is not just a problem in psychotherapeutic technique, but, much more basically, a theological deficiency.

One reason that crisis intervention theory is weak at this point is that the theology which underlies it is guilt theology whereas Job's sense of fault or wrongness concerned his shame. Objectively, he was guiltless, but subjectively, he felt shame. So, even though he was innocent, he felt there was something terribly wrong with him. The crisis he was going through was profoundly humiliating ("I am so sated with shame") and terribly confusing ("I do not know myself"), two sure signs that his sense of wrongness had to do with shame and not guilt. No assurances from Bildad that Job, personally, was blameless, could have any value to Job in his condition; it was not his guilt, but his shame, that condemned him. Counselees whose sense of wrongness is based on shame need to be approached very differently from those whose wrongness connects to guilt.[23]

Some might argue that the crisis intervention method could be revised to embrace the possibility that a crisis has had a dramatic effect on the counselee's self-perception. But this would certainly complicate the method, and could very well reduce its effectiveness. The great virtue of the method is its clarity, as reflected in its step-by-step procedure. To introduce a new consideration, especially one as profound as this, would surely compromise its effectiveness. Since no single method can be expected to meet all the situations encountered in pastoral care, the more appropriate approach is to find an existing method or devise a new one which would be effective with the situation that Bildad encountered with Job. A different method, not the revision of the crisis intervention method, is the better approach.

COUNSELING ON ETHICAL, VALUE, AND MEANING ISSUES

Clinebell maintains that counseling on ethical, value, and meaning issues "is not just one special type of pastoral counseling. These issues are present, at some level, in all human dilemmas and problems, often in subtle or implicit form."[24] There are, however, some situations where these issues have central importance. In the original version of his textbook, there was a chapter on religious-existential problems that included some discussion of "meaning issues."[25] This chapter has been revised and greatly expanded, reflecting current emphases in practical theology on ethical and value issues as well.

Clinebell expresses regret that the ministry of reconciliation has been underemphasized in some mainstream Protestant denominations, mainly as an overreaction against sterile moralism. Its neglect has been reinforced by permissive counseling theories. Counseling concerned with ethical, value, and meaning issues promises to revive the ministry of reconciliation, though such revival depends, in Clinebell's judgment, on our willingness to give more serious attention to the issue of guilt. For Clinebell, the question is how we may take guilt as seriously as its destructive effects warrant without reverting to the legalistic moralism which was appropriately rejected by an earlier generation of pastoral counselors and practical theologians. He maintains that the problem we now confront is to "discover effective methods of resolving guilt and helping people develop constructive consciences."[26]

As a start, we need to understand the whole array of *conscience problems* that people bring to us. There are at least six types of these:

1. consciences with appropriate guilt

2. consciences troubled by neurotic guilt
3. self-righteous consciences
4. underdeveloped or crippled consciences lacking appropriate guilt
5. underdeveloped consciences lacking an appropriate sense of social responsibility and social guilt
6. consciences with value and meaning emptiness

In Clinebell's view, the first question we need to ask is whether the guilt is appropriate or neurotic: "Objectively, appropriate guilt stems from any behavior that actually damages or diminishes the wholeness of persons—oneself or others. Subjectively, appropriate guilt is associated with harm to persons resulting from the misuse of whatever degree of inner freedom one possesses in that situation."[27] In contrast, neurotic guilt feelings result mainly from violating internalized parental prohibitions. They often involve minor or insignificant ethical issues, angry feelings, and aggressive impulses, or sexual fantasies and impulses. Neurotic guilt feelings are compulsive and therefore lacking in the freedom that is present in any genuine ethical choice; and they are chronic, persisting even when the individual is not engaging in the prohibited behavior. In many counselees, appropriate guilt and neurotic guilt feelings are intertwined. But the neurotic elements may be identified by these characteristics:

1. They do not respond to a confession-forgiveness process, but are held onto obsessively.
2. They focus on relatively insignificant ethical issues, or on fantasies and impulses.
3. They seldom motivate constructive amends or long-term changes in the guilt-producing behavior.
4. They may produce masochistic satisfactions.

Given our interest in Job, Clinebell's proposals for the healing of neurotic guilt are not directly relevant. There is not much evidence that Job is suffering from neurotic guilt. He is not obsessed with relatively unimportant ethical issues, or with fantasies and impulses. He exhibits angry emotions, both toward his counselors and God, but these are specific to the situation and are not chronic. He is not masochistic. On the contrary, his pain has been inflicted upon him from without, and he derives no satisfactions from it.

The two categories of underdeveloped consciences are also of no real relevance to Job. They concern individuals who have weak consciences—an irresponsible character structure—or narrow consciences—a well-developed conscience on personal and interpersonal issues but an underdeveloped sense of responsibility on issues of social injustice. Neither of these apply to Job. He is anything but irresponsible. He was deeply offended by his counselors' charges of his alleged inhumanity to the unfortunate: "For I rescued the poor who cried out and the orphan who had no deliverer. I received the blessing of the dying and I brought a song to the heart of the widow. I was eyes to the blind and feet to the lame. I was father to the needy and investigated the case of the stranger" (29:11-13, 15-16). A man who makes these claims, even if they are under dispute, has a developed sense of social responsibility and social guilt.

The remaining conscience problems do have direct bearing on this case. They include an appropriately guilty conscience, a self-righteous conscience, and a conscience of value and meaning emptiness. Appropriate guilt can be addressed therapeutically through a five-stage process: confrontation, confession, forgiveness, restitution and the changing of destructive behavior, and reconciliation. This process is "the path from alienation (from oneself, others, and God) caused by guilt to the reconciliation of completed forgiveness."[28] The critical stage in the process is the point where confrontation by the counselor enables self-confrontation to occur, and the counselee acknowledges that he or she has engaged in behavior that is hurtful to self and others. Such self-confrontation should lead spontaneously to confession, restitution, and changing the destructive behavior pattern that produced the original hurt or harm. Only when such restitution and behavioral change is initiated can we claim that reconciliation has occurred.

People with self-righteous consciences rarely seek pastoral help for their own problems. If they initiate contact at all, it is usually to ask for help in correcting the behavior of a family member, or to criticize the pastor or someone in the congregation for not measuring up to their perfectionist standards. Self-righteousness is a symptomatic defense, a way of trying to "reinforce shaky self-esteem by a sense of moral superiority."[29] By seeing others as ethically and religiously inferior, such people avoid experiencing their deep feelings of self-rejection and self-judgment. Until they sense their need for help, it is virtually impossible to help self-righteous people soften and humanize their defensive consciences. This happens when they become aware of the exorbitant price they pay for their self-righteousness "in the distancing of others and in their own loneliness and lack of joy."[30]

What about the conscience of value and meaning emptiness? Clinebell draws heavily on the writings of Viktor Frankl to explore this conscience problem. Noting that many people suffer from a "chronic existential depression" reflecting "a lack of any dynamic meaning or moving purpose in their lives," he attributes their problems to the frustration of their basic "will to meaning." For Frankl, and for pastoral counselors who use his logotherapy, the root problem of the people they counsel is a profound emptiness in the area of meanings and values. Other problems in living are symptoms of this vacuum. The counselor's task is to "help persons find a motivating meaning for their lives in one or more of three kinds of values—*creative* values, doing something worthwhile; *experiential* values, derived from experiencing something satisfying such as a sunset, a good marriage, the fragrance of a flower, a precious memory, the smile of a friend; and *attitudinal* values, taking a constructive attitude toward whatever situation one is in, even the worst."[31] Frankl views the religious person as one who "says 'yes' to life ... who, in spite of everything that life brings, still faces existence with a basic conviction of the worthwhileness of life."[32] For Clinebell, two ingredients are essential for a meaningful life. One is an "open, energizing relationship with God" and the other is "a dynamic commitment to a cause that is larger than one's circle of self-centered concerns."[33] The discovery or recovery of a meaningful life may begin with one's relationship with God or through commitment to a cause, but inevitably, one will activate the other.

How does the pastoral counselor assist the counselee to regain a sense of life's meaning? The first task is to diagnose the problem accurately as the loss or lack of meaning. When counselees talk directly about aging and death, about their relationship to God or lack of one, or about their ultimate concerns, one can readily discern that they are struggling with the meaning and purpose of their lives. But often the problem of meaning is more difficult to identify. The cry for help is disguised as a dull purposelessness or empty longing, or is hidden behind the face of depression or talk of suicidal thoughts and feelings. So, the desire for meaning often comes in camouflaged form, in behavior reflecting an exaggerated or studied purposelessness, or in longings that are subtly disclosed as the counselee disclaims any desire to recover a sense of life's purpose.

Next, the counselor applies the two focal points of pastoral counseling: the immediate problem in living, and the "ground" of all one's problems. The counselor who helps a person handle the immediate problem more adequately has done only half the job. The other half is "to help him release his humanity and to stimulate his growth on the vertical plane of his life" or to aid him in accepting "the responsibilities and opportunities of authentic being in the world."[34] To open this other half, the counselor may ask such questions as "Does your personal religion seem to be related to this problem, as you see it?" or "How do you see this decision, in the light of what's important, in the long run, in your life?" In this way, the pastor seeks to locate the counselee's problem within a religious frame of reference.

Third, the counselor may use confrontation to challenge counselees who lack awareness of any significant meaning in their lives. The "pastoral counselor should not be timid about raising questions of human destiny." The counselor's task, in fact, is to "help people ask and seek meaningful answers to the 'big questions'—'What does my life mean?' 'Why am I here?' 'What is my relation to the All?' " These questions are always on the counselee's mind but often out of conscious awareness. If they can be raised to consciousness, the counselee will be able "to confront his existential anxiety and to incorporate it into his self-awareness."[35] Such questions may seem abstract or irrelevant to the immediate problem, but they are a *pastoral* counselor's greatest concern, and he or she has a moral obligation to raise them. Says Rollo May: "The therapist is doing the patient a disservice if he takes away from him the realization that it is entirely within the realm of possibility that he forfeit or lose his existence," and that this may be precisely "what he is doing at this very moment."[36]

Zophar as Ethical, Value, and Meaning Counselor

We have seen that Eliphaz and Bildad tried to persuade Job to "commit" his case to God, but that Job refused to do so. His refusal was frustrating to them, and their conversations with him took an increasingly adversarial tone. But it was Zophar who dramatically escalated their adversarial nature by directly accusing Job of personal wrongdoing. He begins with the observation that although Job speaks many words, this does not make him right (11:2). In fact, his boasting, mockery and self-righteous attitude may silence others, and thereby silence the truth (11:3-4). Then Zophar drops his bombshell: "Know that God exacts from you *less* than your guilt demands" (11:6).

This is a double indictment. In the first place, it accuses Job of guilt and rejects his claim to innocence. In the second place, it rejects Job's view that he is God's victim. The truth about God is not that God has some hidden desire to spy on mortals, as Job alleges, but that God has a merciful side which may go unrecognized but is certainly operative in this particular case, for God has not exacted from Job what his guilt demands. Had God wanted to inflict greater suffering on Job, this would have been completely and thoroughly justified.

How fallacious, then, is Job's contention that he has come to know some terrible truths about God—about the vicious, vindictive, and sadistic ways of God! Job knows nothing of the kind! The mystery of God is beyond human knowing (11:7). It is higher than heaven, deeper than Sheol, wider than earth, and broader than sea (11:8-9). Job is wrong to characterize God's hiddenness as duplicity or malevolence. On the nearer side of God's hiddenness, we find an unanticipated mercy and compassion. Of the farther side of God's hiddenness, we must not speak at all. But may we not assume that this inaccessible dimension of God is congruent with the more accessible side of God's hiddenness?

On a more practical level, though, Zophar is certain that Job's talk about God is just a smokescreen, enabling him to distract his counselors from the real issue: his resistance to the disclosure of his own hidden—and profoundly sinful—self. When Job complains that God is a "Seeing Eye" who wants to see whether he will sin (10:14), Zophar defends God on the grounds that "When God sees evil, can God not discern it?" God does not go randomly in search of sin, but like an expert in surveillance, searches where evil is likely to be found. If Job is the object of God's watchful eye, it is because he has something to hide.

Having asserted that Job is truly guilty, Zophar spells out the conditions he must meet to be restored to God's favor. Unlike the recommendations of Eliphaz and Bildad, these conditions are based on the assumption that Job is guilty. A transformation in Job's life is possible if he reorders his mind, stretches out his hands to God in humble obedience, removes evil from his life, and drops the deceit that is evident from the words he has spoken to his friends (11:13-14). If Job will do this, then he will lift his face, free from blemish. He will be secure and unafraid. He will forget his misery and recall it as water flowing past. His world will rise brighter than noon, its darkness will be like morning. He will trust because there is hope. He will search and rest securely (11:15-18).

In short, Zophar believes that Job is guilty but unable to acknowledge appropriate guilt for his plight. Instead, he has resorted to self-righteousness, attributing his problems to God, and this hampers his ability to acknowledge his guilt. Therefore, Zophar's counseling efforts center on persuading Job to acknowledge his guilt. In spelling out the four conditions Job must meet in order to be restored to God's favor (i.e., ordering his mind, reaching out to God in humble obedience, removing evil from his life, and giving up his deceitful ways toward his friends), Zophar's appeal is essentially the same as the five-stage process Clinebell advocates for the healing of appropriate guilt. The problem was that Job, confronting himself, could not see the sin that Zophar attributed to him. Maybe there was something he did as a youth which God is holding against him, but why would this come up now, so many years later, when he can no longer recall what these transgressions might have been? (13:16). To Zophar, this admission to youthful sins is sheer dissimulation, evidence that Job has no desire or intention to discover his sins. If his sins are going to be discovered, Zophar will have to do it without Job's help.

Zophar implies that Job oppressed and abandoned the poor, seizing houses he did not build (20:19). As one commentator points out: "Attitudes and actions toward the underprivileged is a fundamental gauge of integrity and righteousness in Job. Exploitation of the poor was the cruelest accusation [his counselors] could have directed at Job. In his final testimony, Job spends more time defending his treatment of the disenfranchised than any other activity in his life. The touchstone of true 'evil' is oppression of the weak."[37]

But does Zophar's accusation have any merit? Is there any basis for it? Surely, the author wants us to understand that he has made a wrong diagnosis. It is not that Job refuses to admit his guilt, but that his sufferings are inexplicable. This does not mean that the five-step model of reconciliation is itself discredited. But it does mean that its use in this instance is terribly inappropriate.

Is there, then, any basis for Zophar's contention that Job is guilty of self-righteousness? There are reasons that it might appear to be justified. One is that self-righteousness is a symptomatic defense, a way of trying to "reinforce shaky self-esteem by a sense of moral superiority." Job had suffered a series of blows to his self-esteem, having lost his social position, his physical health, the respect of his household, and the affection of his wife. We could imagine that his refusal to acknowledge any guilt was an attempt to maintain what self-esteem he still possessed. Another reason is that his claims to innocence are having the very same interpersonal and emotional effects on him that self-righteousness typically has—"the distancing of others" and the feeling of "loneliness and lack of joy."

But just because Job reacted to his sufferings as a self-righteous person might, and just because his claims to innocence were having the same effects as self-righteousness has, does not mean that he was a self-righteous person. These reactions and effects could instead reflect a value and meaning emptiness. By insisting that Job was guilty and attributing his claims of innocence to a self-righteous conscience, Zophar missed the obvious fact that Job was experiencing a meaning vacuum.

What Job exhibits throughout his conversations with his three friends is value and meaning emptiness. Again and again he contends that there is no reason for him to continue to live. Life no longer has any meaning for him, and he laments the fact that he had ever been born. He lacks the two ingredients necessary for a meaningful life: "an open, energizing relationship with God" and "a dynamic commitment to a cause that is larger than one's circle of self-centered concerns." Throughout these conversations, he is a man who doubts the value of life. Why be virtuous in a world where there is no higher moral order? Why entertain the belief that life has meaning when one is visited with gratuitous and meaningless suffering? Call this "existential anxiety," the frustration of one's "will to meaning," or a sense that "life has been emptied of all meaning and purpose." Whatever we call it, this is Job's condition. He is suffering from an empty conscience, perceiving that it does not really matter whether he does right or wrong, is responsible or irresponsible, keeps or breaks promises, speaks truth or tells lies, lives or dies. Where evil is tolerated on earth and in heaven, and where wrongdoers are not punished, either in life or in death, where are the ultimate norms and standards by which we order our lives and make claims for the meaning of our existence?

The Theology of Ethical, Value, and Meaning Counseling

Zophar misdiagnosed Job's situation. He viewed Job as guilty and tried to get him to confess his guilt, make restitution, and seek reconciliation with God and with those whom he had allegedly wronged. When Job refused to confess his guilt, Zophar attributed his refusal to self-righteousness.

What if Zophar had not misdiagnosed Job's situation? What if he had, in fact, approached Job as a counselee who was suffering from a meaning vacuum? What might he have done to help Job overcome his empty conscience? One approach would be to act on Frankl's proposal that we help such persons find a motivating meaning for their lives through one of three kinds of value. Job could be encouraged to do something worthwhile (creative value). He could be invited to identify satisfying experiences in his life, such as a sunset, a good marriage, or a precious memory (experiential value). He could be challenged to adopt a constructive view of his situation, no matter how hopeless it seemed (attitudinal value).

If Zophar were to take this approach, his best prospects for success would, no doubt, involve helping Job to take a more positive attitude toward life. Being infirm and a social pariah, Job was not very well situated to do something worthwhile. Because satisfying experiences were hard to find in his condition (the fragrance of a flower was obliterated by the stench of his own body), and past experiences were difficult to recall in the midst of his agony and torment, it would be difficult to appeal to his sense of experiential value. Zophar's best hope for success would be in helping Job to take a constructive attitude toward his very tragic situation. This approach would mean helping him become a "religious" person again, one who "says 'yes' to life," and "in spite of everything that life brings, still faces existence with a basic conviction of the worthwhileness of life."

But how would Zophar go about this? What approach would he take to help Job acquire a positive attitude toward his situation? According to Clinebell, the counselor's role in meaning-vacuum counseling involves confronting the counselee with the "big questions": What does my life mean? Why am I here? What is my relation to the All? But Job is already asking these big questions, and asking them only deepens his meaning vacuum. Eliphaz says that Job should take comfort—find meaning?—in the knowledge that his life was spared. To Job, however, the question is "Why did I not die at birth, come forth from the womb and expire? Why were there knees to welcome me, or breasts for me to suck? For now I would be lying in repose, I would be asleep, resting in peace" (3:11-13).

The method of ethical, value, and meaning counseling has enabled us to diagnose Job's condition as a meaning vacuum. But having helped us in this regard, the method is not very useful for alleviating the problem. How does one help a person in Job's condition take a constructive attitude toward life, especially when this person is unable to do anything worthwhile and has no satisfying experiences to savor? Here the method leaves us dangling. It is useful for diagnostic purposes, but vague in showing how to help this individual regain a meaningful existence. By its own admission this is a theological deficiency; the issue is how to help the individual become a "religious" person again, one who is able to say "yes" to life in spite of everything that life has done to him.

If the crisis intervention method failed to take adequate account of the effects of victimization on Job's own self-perception, the meaning-counseling method gives little guidance for alleviating the corresponding effects of dehumanization. When a person is no longer able to do anything worthwhile and no longer has satisfying experiences to contemplate, he or she is being dehumanized, deprived of the fundamental qualities of human existence that have allowed us to claim that we are created in the image of God. We cannot expect a counseling method to provide all the answers a pastoral counselor needs for reversing such dehumanization, but we have a right to expect that it will offer some practical guidance toward this end.

The reframing method does not have all the answers, either. But it is an especially effective therapeutic intervention with persons for whom life has lost its meaning. Viktor Frankl, whose logotherapy focuses on meaning loss, frequently used the reframing method. It is no exaggeration to say that this method was inspired, to a significant degree, by Frankl's technique of paradoxical intention. Watzlawick's own debt to Frankl is revealed in his account of Frankl's work with a counselee whose life lost all meaning after the death of his wife:

> Life has lost its meaning; everything that was beautiful and worth living for has left this world together with the deceased—and within this frame only the return of the dead could again lend sense to one's own life. Frankl reframes the situation by asking the patient to imagine that, while Frankl cannot of course bring the deceased back to life, he would introduce him to another person who not only physically but also otherwise resembles the dead person in every respect; who is so completely informed about the life of the deceased that together they would be able to recall and discuss every detail of their joint experiences— would the patient accept this person as a valid substitute? In attempting to answer this question, the patient is forced to look at his loss from a perspective that lies outside the vicious, closed circle of his grief. Frankl reports that his patient usually rejects the illusionary alternative, and it seems to be that in achieving this rejection Frankl has produced a decisive change in the patient's world image: He has gently brought the sufferer closer to accepting the irreversibility of the beloved person's death and thereby has created some distance to it.[38]

Forcing the patient to look at his loss from a perspective that lies outside the vicious, closed circle of his grief: This is reframing, and this, we will see, is what God forced Job to do.

CONCLUSION

If the pastoral counseling methods explored in this chapter were exotic and rarely used, the knowledge that they were ineffective would be easy to dismiss. But these are the methods most commonly used by pastors. Because they were ineffective with Job, they are likely to be ineffective with people who identify their situations with that of Job. The enormous popularity of Rabbi Harold S. Kushner's *When Bad Things Happen to Good People* shows that vast numbers of persons identify with Job.[39] Does this mean that pastors are helpless to do anything in behalf of these people? Are pastors but "worthless physicians?" (13:4).

Surely we need not resign ourselves to such a fate. Instead, we need to think more critically than we usually do about *why* our methods are ineffective with certain individuals. I submit that the major reason our most commonly used methods fail is that they are status quo methods. They are designed to help people be as they were before calamity struck. To put it another way, these methods are designed for first-order change.

If this is so, why assume they would be effective with people whose views of God, of self, and of life in this world are undergoing radical change, people who are certain they will never be as they were before? These people are experiencing the pain, but also the challenge, of second-order change—of change in the very system of life itself. They have no desire to return to their prior state within the status quo, and why should they? In his praise of people of faith who voluntarily made themselves strangers and exiles on earth, the author of Hebrews points out: "If they had been thinking of that land from which they had gone out, they would have had opportunity to return. But as it is, they desire a better country." (11:15-16).

The Jobs of this world could go back if they wanted to. But why? Eliphaz, Bildad, and Zophar represent the pull of the status quo, the return to normal. Job epitomizes the human longing for something more—a radically new awareness of God, of self, of world. To the exponent of the unchanged state, Job's new awarenesses were bad, sick, and empty, the very kiss of death. But Job did not see it this way. Instead, he vigorously defended his integrity against his counselors' efforts to prove how sick and perverse he had become. And the integrity he defended was that of the *new* Job—victimized, dehumanized, and radicalized—emerging from the ashes of the status quo. This was the Job they were unable to take seriously, the Job their counseling methods permitted them to ignore.

CHAPTER SEVEN
God Reframes
for Second-Order
Change

After Job's counselors gave up their efforts to counsel him, God intervened, and through this intervention, succeeded where they had failed. Why was God successful?

Some have suggested that God succeeded just because God is God, that God is able to achieve whatever God wills. Others have maintained that God had success because profound changes will inevitably occur in individuals who have experienced God in some direct and overpowering way. Still others contend that God was successful because God actually spoke to Job, and said things to him which enabled him to see matters differently. To such observers, it was the actual content of God's response—the words which God spoke—that was responsible for the change in Job.

Most commentators on the book of Job believe that the third view is the one to which its author subscribes. That Job was not changed immediately when God appeared but only after God had spoken to him at length indicates that the mere appearance of God—however overwhelming this must have been—was not the decisive factor. What God actually said to Job was the critical element.

Therefore, we are concerned here with what God said to Job, contrasting what God said to what was said by Job's counselors. I am convinced that God's response to Job was an instance of reframing, and that God succeeded with Job because this reframing produced a second-order change.

GOD'S RESPONSE TO JOB

The First Response: Job's Integrity Confirmed

God's response to Job consists of two parts. The first part (38:1—40:5) begins on a threatening note: "Who is this who clouds my design in darkness, presenting arguments without knowledge? Gird your loins like a hero; I will ask questions and you will inform me" (38:2-3). Then God poses a series of questions which challenge Job to demonstrate firsthand knowledge of the creation of the earth and sea, the location of the underworld, and the heavenly spheres: "Where were you when I laid the earth's foundations? Tell me if you have gained discernment! Who fixed its dimensions? Surely you know!" (38:4). Has Job "penetrated the storehouses of snow?" (38:22). Does he know "the way for dispersing lightning?" (38:24). And what about the stars? "Can you bind the fetters of the Pleiades or loose the reins of Orion?" (38:30-31). "Do you know the laws of heaven? Can you establish its order on earth?" (38:33). Of course, Job does not respond to this opening volley of questions. What could he have said?

God turns next to the animal kingdom and asks: "Can you hunt for the lion, and appease the appetite of whelps when they crouch in their dens and lie in wait in their lair?" (38:39-40). "Who provides prey for the raven, when its fledglings cry out to God, wandering about without any food?" (38:41-42). "Do you watch over the calving of hinds? Can you count the months they must fulfill? Do you know the time of their delivery, when they crouch to deliver their young and drop their offspring?" (39:1-3). "And who set the wild ass free?" (39:5). "And will the wild ox serve you, spending the night beside your crib, harrowing the valleys behind you, harvesting your grain, and gathering it in from the threshing floor?" (39:9-12). Continuing this inventory of living creatures, God asks Job about the stupidity and majesty of the ostrich, the power of the horse, the soaring of the hawk, and the bloodthirstiness of the eagle. Again, Job has nothing to say in response.

Then, aware that Job has threatened litigation against God, challenging God to meet him in a court of law, God asks with withering sarcasm: "Will the one with a suit against God correct me? Will the one arraigning God answer me?" To this, Job finally responds: "Behold, I am small; how can I refute you? I clap my hands on my mouth. I have spoken once, I cannot answer. Twice, and will do so no more" (40:4-5). And so ends the first part of God's response to Job.

What is going on here? What is God really saying to Job, and what is happening between them? One commentator sees this part of God's response as an ironic fulfillment of Job's expectations.[1] God's appearance in the whirlwind was a fulfillment of Job's anticipation that God would in fact respond to his summons, but this appearance was not what Job expected. Job had set down certain conditions for his meeting with God. His first condition was that God would resist the impulse to terrorize him so that he would not be intimidated about speaking to God. In fact, God did not overtly terrorize him with this response, but God certainly intimidated him with these confounding, rhetorical questions. Job's second condition was that God would summon him and that Job would respond to God's charges, or, alternatively, Job would state his case and God would then try to refute it. Clearly, God chose the first option of summoning Job, but then did not proceed at all as Job had expected. God did not inform Job of the charges against him, as Job had requested. Instead, the whole issue of Job's alleged guilt was completely ignored.

Job's request for a meeting with God was technically honored, but on God's terms and not his. God put questions to Job, but Job had no answers for them because they were not the questions he had expected; in any case, they were impossible to answer in any intelligent or intelligible way. They had no connection whatever to Job's alleged sins and wrongdoings. They were clever rhetorical questions and riddles—matters which required esoteric knowledge. They threw Job completely off guard because they had absolutely nothing to do with what Job had assumed to be the point of contention between himself and God. Job was prepared to defend his integrity before God, to make a case for his innocence, to clear himself of any charges. But God ignored all this. Job's innocence or guilt was seemingly not an issue for God. I believe this was because God perceived that Job's real problem was not his resistance to confessing guilt—as Zophar had alleged—but his deep and pervasive sense of life's meaninglessness. I will return to this point later.

God's failure to address the issues which had so exercised Job and his three counselors leads the same commentator to note that God's response to Job was a thematic shock. There is no link between God's response to Job and the conversations which had preceded it; the issue of the relationship between sin and suffering—such a central theme of the counseling dialogues—is not even mentioned in God's response to Job. Nor is the question of Job's integrity directly addressed. Instead, according to this commentator, the basic theme of the first half of God's response to Job is the integrity of *God* as the creator of a complex world![2] This defense of God's integrity turns on the idea that the created world, and everything within it, is thoroughly paradoxical. When the lion's whelps and raven's fledglings cry to God for food, what is God to do? If they are not provided food, surely they will starve. If God makes prey available to them, the prey become innocent victims. The challenge which underlies God's response is this: Could you, Job, do any better? Are you able to create a world in which there are no innocent victims?

If the content of God's response was a thematic shock, it did, according to this commentator, have structural integrity. The various segments of the response reinforced one another, showing that God's design for the cosmos is a meticulously controlled network of structures and processes.[3] This network includes the world's extremities—the heavens above, the nether world beneath, and the earth between. Its complexity is reflected in the interaction between the spheres, especially as the heavens relate to earth, and sustains human life; and its meticulous control is reflected in God's governance of the animal kingdom, which is a threat to human society, but is also threatened by it. As humans will not accept servitude to wild animals, so the animals will not be subdued by human masters. The wild ass is a case in point for "he laughs at the furor of the city and hears no shouts from a taskmaster" (39:7). Thus, the animal world and human society are marching to the tunes of different drummers, and neither would survive if God did not protect the freedom of the one against the freedom of the other.

Paradox, not rational order, sets the tone for this portrayal of the cosmos as a meticulously controlled network of structures and processes. The various orders of the world do not interact in rational, logical ways, but play off one another in constantly shifting patterns of interaction. This is why the design of the cosmos is beyond human knowledge. Its network of relationships is surprising—as unexpected and irrational as God's appearance to Job in a whirlwind. An especially striking example of the paradox inherent in the very structure of the world is the ostrich. She is very stupid, leaving her eggs where they can be crushed, and treating her young as though they are not her own. Yet, she is also proud and majestic, "with gracious plumage and pinions," as she "rears up on high" and "laughs at horse and rider" (39:13-18). In a word, she is a living paradox, a combination of stupidity and grace, idiocy and grandeur. Thus, where Elihu had emphasized God's absolute power to create and guide the world and make it do God's bidding (36:22—37:13), this speech emphasizes the governance of the world as involving competing claims, a pattern of checks and balances, a loss here to effect a gain there. There is design in the cosmic order and God is in control of it; yet we should not look for rational order, but instead note its many paradoxes.

So, God did not address the themes and issues that were so hotly discussed by Job and his counselor friends. Yet, in noting the paradoxical nature of the universe, God indirectly addressed Job's situation. If the world itself is inherently paradoxical, then it should not be surprising that a blameless man suffers and a wicked man goes to his grave happy and contented. If the world were rationally ordered, this would not happen. But the order of the world is paradox, which is not disorder or sheer chaos, but a curious kind of order. It is the order reflected in the ostrich, whose life is paradoxical to the core: how can a bird who is so stupid and insensitive be so gracious and proud?

Because it addresses Job's situation only indirectly, God's response to Job is akin to a parable. With parables, issues are not addressed directly; instead, considerable burden is placed upon the listener to discern the story's relevance to the matter at hand. Since God makes no direct reference to Job's sufferings, his alleged guilt, his allegations against God, or his desire to take God to court, the response seems irrelevant. But when viewed as a parable, the speech is an indirect response to all that has gone on before, for its basic theme—the paradoxical nature of the world—is profoundly relevant to Job's situation: not just the paradox of a righteous man suffering while a wicked one flourishes, but the deeper paradox that the righteous man *knows* he is righteous but *feels* he is not.

The parable of the ostrich points to the parabolic nature of God's response as a whole; more to the point, it is an indirect commentary on Job himself.[4] The very fact that the ostrich is a bird that cannot fly implies a close analogy between this bird and mortals—closer, certainly, than the hawk or the eagle. At first, the ostrich flourishes, as her wings rejoice, revealing gracious plumage and pinions. But she leaves her eggs where they can be crushed and trampled, and treats her young harshly, as though they were not hers. This is not due to evil intent but because she lacks wisdom and discernment. And yet, in spite of her inability to conduct herself as wisely as she (or we) might wish, she is an undeniably impressive bird as she rears up and startles a horse and rider (39:13-18).

If this parable, or parable-within-a-parable, is intended for Job so that he might see himself mirrored in the ostrich, its point is surely not that Job is guilty; but neither is he in a position to be unambiguously proud of himself. For all his impressive qualities, and they are many, he has personal characteristics which are less than impressive—which are, in fact, evidence of gross stupidity. Such stupidity is not a matter of guilt, or reason to repent, but it certainly warrants his notice and awareness. Job is not nearly so wise as he thinks he is.

Some readers see in the ostrich's disregard for her young a veiled reference to Job's sin against his children, an allegation that was broached by Zophar, alluding to the wicked man whose sons were left to the mercy of the poor (20:10).[5] But the parable's relevance to Job does not depend on these alleged biographical links. Its application to Job has nothing to do with him as a unique personality but as a representative of the human race—an inherently paradoxical species: majestic yet cruel, resourceful yet stupid. Also, the point of the parable is not that the ostrich knowingly sinned against her young and is therefore blameworthy. On the contrary, God admits to having "deprived her of wisdom and withheld her portion of discernment" (39:17).

So, God has not come to castigate or to humiliate Job. On the contrary, God observes that the ostrich, because she is such a paradox, is an interesting and appealing bird. As she rears on high and laughs at horse and rider, can we not see in this behavior

Job's own bravado and disregard for personal safety as he flung his insults at God Almighty? Even as God accepts the ostrich as a valued member of the created world, so God accepts Job, a mixture of grandeur and stupidity. He could have gotten himself into very deep trouble if God were one to carry a grudge. But how could the creator and sustainer of the ostrich carry a grudge against a man such as Job, as he rears up on high and flings his pathetic insults? Only the most intensely singleminded and obsessively goal-oriented rider would fail to notice the ostrich alongside the road, and only the most dully serious and stolid rider would not return her laugh.

Thus, in affirming the integrity of his own ways, God, indirectly, affirmed the integrity of Job's ways. God did not hold Job up as a paragon of virtue, or commend him as an exemplary mortal, but God did affirm Job's basic integrity, just as God affirmed the ways of the ostrich. Job has behaved as he was created to behave, and has performed acceptably, as mortals go.

Our question, of course, is whether God's response to Job was a reframing. While this question can best be answered after we have reviewed the whole response, a preliminary judgment based on the first half of God's response shows that this part is certainly a reframing. Notice that God used not one, but a number of the reframing techniques described in chapter 2.

The technique of *dereflection* recognizes that self-examination leads to healthy self-assessment, but that exaggerated self-observation can be harmful. To counteract hyper-reflection, the counselor cannot just advise the counselee not to think so much about a certain subject; this advice simply draws attention to it. The strategy of dereflection involves getting counselees to think of something else, thus detaching them from their symptoms and directing them to another, more positive subject. This direction typically involves asking clients to think of desirable, positive, and healthy activities which would enrich their lives.

God uses this technique of dereflection in response to Job. Job's sufferings are not alluded to at all; the question of his responsibility for his sufferings, which so concerned his counselors, is likewise ignored. Also deflected was the whole question of the meaning of Job's sufferings, that is, their possible disciplinary value. Instead, God shifted the entire focus from Job and his troubles to the world and its many interesting—and paradoxical—phenomena. Notice, too, that God did not divert Job's attention from himself by focusing on the social world, as Job had done in his complaint that God "makes counselors wander naked and makes judges go mad" (12:17). Instead, God focused on the world of nature, and commented on *its* startling and puzzling features.

Job, of course, was well aware that the behavior of birds and animals provides insights into the human world. He would know that God's references to the natural world were not irrelevant to the human situation of which he had spoken so passionately in his conversations with the three counselors. Still, by shifting the focus from the human to the natural world, God took Job's mind off his own negative ruminations and forced him to think about less depressing things. In effect, God arrested the process of Job's dehumanization by opening the door to new experiences. Knowing that Job's self-reflections had led only to hopelessness, despair, and a sense of life's utter meaninglessness, God led Job to begin thinking about the world outside himself, about experiential values. Through the technique of dereflection, God began the process of restoring Job's sense that life has meaning. At a certain point, self-reflection can become self-defeating, and a well executed distraction, as God's was, can effect a dramatic change in attitude. God's talk about the world forced Job to think about something besides himself, and this was clearly therapeutic.

Dereflection was God's primary reframing technique, but there were others. The *confusion* technique involves prefacing an especially important therapeutic intervention with a deliberately confusing statement. Unnerved by this statement, the counselee welcomes and responds positively to the counselor's next statement, greeting it with considerable relief. The counselee may also be more inclined to devise his or her own solutions to a problem after being subjected to much fumbling and tendentious discourse from the counselor.

In context, God's rhetorical statements at the beginning of the response to Job are quite confusing. Job had anticipated that God would begin by stating the charges against him. Instead, God began by asking Job where he was when God laid the earth's foundations. God's questions were rhetorical, and therefore unanswerable, but they were also confusing because they were not what Job had expected. By using this technique, God utterly disarmed Job; he was prepared for a debate with God, and was instead confronted with a barrage of unanswerable questions, many of which seemed pointless and irrelevant.

If confusing statements are made to set the stage for the intervention which follows, what, in this case, was the intervention? What God wanted Job to hear, but suspected that he would not be able to hear unless the way were prepared for it, was that God did not consider Job to be guilty of anything; on the contrary, God affirmed Job's integrity. Would Job have heard this if God had said it straightaway? I doubt it. Consumed by his anger, he would have mistrusted this affirmation, questioning God's motives for saying it. An angry Job could not have heard God's affirmation, but a confused Job could hear it, because hearing it would reduce his sense of confusion. By the time God told the parable of the ostrich, Job was desperate for some sense of clarity, some meaningful connection between what God was saying and what Job was experiencing. The parable in this context was clear and transparent: "There's nothing wrong with you, Job, so get on with your life."

A third technique that God uses in response to Job is the technique of *benevolent sabotage.* Here, the person who would like to influence the other is in no position to demand, much less force the other's compliance. The technique of benevolent sabotage involves taking a *one-down* position, based on the frank admission that one is unable to control the other's behavior. With this admission, the other quickly finds that assertion and defiance make little sense; he or she is much more likely to be cooperative. God uses benevolent sabotage by acknowledging that the world is complex, and that it is difficult to see how innocent victimization could be eliminated. God does not claim to preside over a perfect system, and, in this way, takes a one-down position. This action places the burden on Job to show how *he* would govern any better. Job is, of course, aware that he would be incapable of doing so. Therefore, Job's assertive and defiant attitude is abandoned, replaced by an attitude of increased respect for God and for the difficulties that God confronts in attempting to govern the world in a wise and equitable manner. If God had not taken this one-down position, Job would have continued in his challenge and defiance of God.

Thus, in the first part of God's response to Job, at least three reframing techniques were used. God did not terrorize Job, but instead used subtler methods. Although somewhat devious, they were not used for purposes of manipulation and control; on the contrary, they were designed to free Job from his self-destructive anger and despair, and to get him to reinvest in life. Of course, Job's answer to this intervention is disappointing to us, as he was able only to affirm his "smallness." He was beginning to respond, emotionally and attitudinally, but his words did not yet reflect this change. So God continued the therapeutic process that was now under way, addressing Job, once again, from the whirlwind.

The Second Response: Job's God-Images Confirmed

In the second response, God again challenged Job to "gird your loins like a hero. I will ask questions and you will inform me!" (40:7). This response has two main parts: God's subjugation of Behemoth, the red hippopotamus, and Leviathan, the crocodile. Both are ferocious and terrifying, and Leviathan is especially fearsome: "His sneezings flash forth lightning. And his eyes are like the eyelids of dawn. Torches issue from his mouth. Flames of fire leap forth. His breath ignites coals. Flame pours from his mouth" (41:18-19, 21). Yet God is able to control the beasts. God draws a sword against Behemoth, "takes him by the mouth with rings" and "pierces his nose with hooks" (40:19, 24). And Leviathan, for all his ferocity when roused, cowers before the face of God (41:10).

This section of the response continues the theme of God's integrity, which was initiated in the first half. By citing the examples of Behemoth and Leviathan, God asks how the limited moral law which Job (generally believed to have been a governor) administered in his own society could possibly be the rule for administering the whole cosmos. As one commentator puts it: "If Job, like Elihu and the friends, believes that God should rule the world by administering according to a rigid law of moral retribution which necessitates the immediate punishment of the wicked and the total destruction of evil by direct intervention, then Job had better demonstrate how it should be done."[6] Obviously, a more flexible approach is needed. God does not destroy the forces of chaos, but does hold them in check. If the cosmos were rationally ordered, these forces would not exist at all. But the cosmos is a paradox, and so we have here a picture of an all-powerful God engaging, nonetheless, in mortal combat against these powerful forces. That God is able to subdue them is a testimony to God's integrity, for surely Job does not for a moment think that he himself could ever restrain these foes, much less subdue them.

Yet, defense of God's own integrity is only one of the major themes of this second part of the response to Job. The other is the affirmation of Job. While Job's allegations of God's dereliction and vindictiveness are rejected, the response, as a whole, does affirm the images which Job attributed to God. Job had viewed God as a Seeing Eye who was constantly trying to discern some hidden fault in Job, and as a Hunter whose intent was to kill him. While these were unflattering, even blasphemous images of God, God affirms these images, albeit in a much more positive way, in responding to Job.

The image of God as Seeing Eye becomes the image of the One who watches the world, and watches over it—a theme especially prominent in the first half of the response that describes God's oversight of the world. God makes a specific allusion to this image with a pointed question: "Do you watch over the calving of hinds?" (39:1). The image of God as Hunter is much more prominent in the second half, where God is portrayed as taking Behemoth by the mouth with rings and piercing his nose with hooks. Then, in noting how God's very look subdues Leviathan, the images of Hunter and Seeing Eye converge.

In contrast, God asserts that Job is neither a good and informed watcher, nor an effective hunter. As watcher, Job does not know the dimensions of the earth, how the lightning is dispersed, how many months it takes for hinds to give birth, or how many clouds there are in the sky. As hunter, Job is hapless before Leviathan: "Can you draw out Leviathan with a hook, or depress his tongue with a cord? Can you put a rope through his nose, or pierce his jaw with a barb?" (41:1-2). Of course not. Furthermore, where would Job be, where would any mortal be, if God were *not* what Job asserts God to be: the Seeing Eye and the Hunter? Yes, says God, I am the Watchful Eye, and it is good for you that I am. Yes, I am the Hunter, and where would you be if I were not? Far from rejecting the images that Job ascribes to God, God embraces them and gives them a positive connotation.

Is it because Job saw that God is Watchful Eye and Hunter that he is acclaimed as having spoken what is "right" about God while his counselor friends are condemned for speaking falsely of God? (42:7). Job may have had a distorted and partial perspective on these images, but they are images with which God identifies because they are critically important to God's design and governance of the world. In a world where ostriches do not recognize their own children, where the lion's whelps and raven's fledglings cry for food, and where the monsters of chaos threaten to overrun the earth and sea, God will continue to be the Seeing Eye and the Hunter, mediating between the world's conflicting claims and interests. If this means that Job will also experience God as the one who looks into his inner self and exposes and attacks his vulnerable spots, this is the price he must pay for his apprehension that God, on the other hand, is watching over him and protecting his life from danger. These two images capture the highly differentiated personality which is God.

Job's answer to God's second response was brief. He acknowledged that God "can do everything, and that no scheme of yours can be thwarted" (42:2). He also admitted that he had spoken "without discernment of things beyond me which I did not know" (42:3). But, then, as though his eyes were now opened, he exclaimed, "I have heard of you with my ears, but now my eyes see you. Therefore I retract and repent of dust and ashes" (42:5-6).

This brief speech has been the subject of much controversy and debate. Some commentators maintain that Job repents of his arrogant attitude and abases himself in humiliation and shame. Others contend that this speech is about reconciliation, not capitulation, as Job acquires a new understanding of God's governance of the world and reaffirms his faith with appropriate humility. Still others assert that Job's confession is tongue-in-cheek, an attempt to mollify an offended and defensive deity with an insincere but self-protective confession of guilt. And some maintain that this speech is a final act of defiance, with Job's "now my eyes see you" to be viewed as uncomplimentary of God, for what Job has seen is a God who, as he had earlier alleged, is unjust, unfeeling, and cruel.

The emerging consensus, however, is that the speech is not an act of self-abasement and not a confession of guilt. The words, "I retract," imply that Job is withdrawing his case of litigation against God, thus signaling that he is dropping his charges. This is very different from the traditional translation of this phrase—"I despise myself"—which suggests a confession of guilt or act of contrition. Also, the words "repent *of* dust and ashes" (as opposed to the traditional "repent *in* dust and ashes") do not imply remorse for his arrogant attitude nor a confession of guilt, but a decision to abandon his status and role as "an isolated sufferer."[7] Thus, "dust and ashes" refers to Job's separation from the community as he sat among the ashes, and he now "repents" of his longing for death and instead chooses to return to his former place within human society. Repentance of dust and ashes may also mean renunciation of mortals' tendency to view themselves as mere creatures ("dust and ashes") rather than co-creators with God.[8] Then, too, repentance of dust and ashes may be seen as the reclamation of the identity of a righteous individual and the decision to set aside the shame and self-doubts which his experience of victimization had caused.

These interpretations of the "repent of dust and ashes" statement, while different in emphasis and nuance, agree that the tone of Job's concluding speech was neither one of self-abasement nor of false contrition or defiance. Job does not admit to being guilty of the sins ascribed to him by his counselor friends, or of arrogance and presumption in the manner in which he talked about God. He acknowledges that he has not always spoken with discernment, that there are many things he knows nothing about, but the general tone of this response is positive, if not triumphant: Job will withdraw his claims against God, will return to human society, will accept his co-creative role with God, and will reclaim, subjectively as well as objectively, his identity as a righteous man. The meaning vacuum which he has been experiencing ever since this awful episode began will be replaced with a new sense of life's meaning and purpose. The rehabilitation of Job is under way and will not be impeded.

The second part of God's speech to Job continued the reframing process begun in the first part. The technique of dereflection continued as God challenged Job to focus his attention on the external world and not on himself and his own inner conflicts. But, where God's first speech encouraged Job to think about experiential values, the second one led him to consider creative values as he began to perceive that God was inviting him to become a co-creator, a partner with God in the governance of the world. As Job began to see himself in the role of co-creator with God, he shed his negative self-image, renounced the dehumanizing effects of his victimization, and returned to human society, determined to do his part to further God's intentions for the world.

God also continued to use the strategy of benevolent sabotage, affirming the images for God which Job had advanced but reinterpreting them so as to deprive Job of his defiance. Putting a very different twist on these images, God forced Job to admit that he very much needed the God whom he had sarcastically described as Seeing Eye and Hunter.

God followed these uses of the dereflection and benevolent sabotage techniques with the *prescription* technique. This involves giving the client a task to perform, a task which may or may not have any direct bearing on the client's actual problems. In this case, God ordered Job to intercede in behalf of his three counselor friends. While this prescription was ostensibly for the purpose of rehabilitating the three friends, its major effect was to solidify the therapeutic gains that Job himself was making. The prescription was based on the assumption that Job had now been accorded co-creator status with God, had renounced his dehumanization, and was prepared to play a constructive role in human society. The prescription helped Job's friends, but it was even more helpful to Job, as it put the attitudinal changes reflected in his response to God into direct and immediate practice.

God's use of these reframing techniques is a clear indication that God's counseling approach to Job was based on the reframing method. Another indication that God used the reframing method is that God devised a treatment plan that flew directly in the face of previous unsuccessful efforts to treat Job. God knew about these previous attempts, knew what they were, and knew that they had only made matters worse. Like all good reframing plans, God's plan took positive advantage of the knowledge that other attempts had been made to help Job and that the stage was set for a radically different approach. Let us now analyze these previous approaches and see how God reframed them, examining first the counselors' attempted solution, and then Job's effort to solve the problem himself.

THE COUNSELORS' ATTEMPTED
SOLUTION

For the purposes of assessing various pastoral counseling methods, we have treated the counselors up to this point as separate individuals. Now that we are concerned with God's reframing method, it is appropriate to view the three counselors as a group and to assess their collective efforts. Why did all three fail? The authors of *Change* would say that they failed because they mishandled Job's difficulty. But how was it mishandled? What was wrong with their approach?

Clearly, their failure was not *simplification,* a failure to take action where the difficulty clearly demanded action. They *did* take action by talking with Job, and the serious way in which they approached their counseling task demonstrated their awareness of the severity of his difficulty. They could see what it was doing to his spirit and tried to help in whatever way they could.

Nor did they simplify by trying a quick-fix solution. They did not offer any miracle cures. They did not offer or prescribe artificial substances to help him forget his troubles. They did not resort to sorcery or magic in a desperate but cynical effort to restore his children, possessions, and health. Job called them quacks, but to their credit, they never resorted to gimmicky solutions to this very difficult and painful situation.

Utopianism, or taking action where it should not have been taken because the situation is essentially unchangeable, was not their error, either. They focused on the aspect of the situation that they *could* help to change—Job's attitude. This behavior shows that they were not utopianists. They did hold out the hope that, through an attitude change, Job would also experience changes in his objective situation. This was not an unreasonable hope because they believed, and had grounds for believing, that God would respond favorably to the attitudinal change they envisioned, and would, on this basis, begin to restore Job to his former health and well-being. Even had they not believed in God's power to heal, such a hope would make sense on purely psychological grounds since a positive attitude can, by itself, lead to significant improvements in one's objective situation.

To be sure, Job, as is common with counselees, accused his counselor friends of utopianism. To him, they were guilty of *projective* utopianism, of believing that certain goals which he considered unattainable—such as changing his fate—were in fact attainable. He also accused them of harboring illusions of originality (12:2-3) and of self-righteousness (12:3), common traits of utopianists. Job's attacks, in turn, produced in them feelings of paranoia, which are also common to projective utopianists. As the counseling process came to an unsuccessful end, they displayed symptoms of personal inadequacy, common to *introjective* utopianists when they have been unable to reach what has proven to be an unattainable goal.

But utopianism is not why the counselors failed. Their basic mistake was the third mishandling of difficulties, the attempt to achieve a first-order change where a second-order change was needed. As they made their various recommendations to Job to seek God, they were unaware that these proposals were inherently *paradoxical*. They were advising him to seek the help of the very one whom he perceived to be responsible for his difficulties. To Job, this was a real paradox; yet they persisted in advising him to seek God even after he had pointed out to them that what they were advocating was paradoxical, placing him in an untenable double bind: How can I seek the help of the one who is causing all my difficulties? This double bind was made worse when his reluctance to turn to God for help was interpreted as personal culpability for his sufferings. The more he resisted what they proposed, the more convinced they were that he was guilty.

Had they been able to recognize the paradox in what they were recommending, they might have been able to appreciate his resistance. They might have seen that the paradoxical, double-binding nature of the action they were asking him to take, rather than any previous actions on his part, or false and deceitful intentions now, was the reason for his resistance. Their basic error was that they used first-order change methods where a second-order change was needed. As we have noted, paradox not recognized as such condemns to first-order change.

JOB'S ATTEMPTED SOLUTION

Frustrated by his counselors' efforts to help him, Job began to formulate his own plan. Unlike theirs, his plan involved awareness of the paradoxical nature of what his counselors were proposing, and acting on this awareness. His idea of litigation against God—meeting God in a court of law—was based on conscious awareness of the paradox—that he would be seeking good from the very one who had wronged him. Of course, he had serious doubts that this solution would work. He had every reason to expect that God would come to this encounter only to mistreat him even more. Also, in contrast to his counselors' proposals, he himself would not be coming to God in a spirit of humility and remorse designed to placate God, for this was something his strong sense of integrity would not allow him to do. From a common-sense point of view, his plan would appear to be a rather poor one, clearly destined to fail.

If Job's plan was based on awareness of the paradox of seeking help from the very one he felt had wronged him, why did it not succeed? The problem was that it left too much to chance. His objective—his own vindication leading to a restored sense of righteousness—was sufficiently precise. But while he laid down conditions for how the court case would proceed, he had no way of ensuring that his adversary would meet these conditions. If his adversary would not comply with them, the plan, as Job well knew, would not succeed. No therapeutic plan, reframing or otherwise, is foolproof, and every plan will have some unanticipated effects or consequences. But Job devised a plan over which he had almost no control. Its success depended on God's willingness to participate in the plan and to play the role devised by Job. But Job had no assurance that he could secure God's participation in the plan, much less that God would participate as Job desired.

Recall Jerry and Sue, the young couple with the domineering parents. The reframing plan was based on the expectation that his parents would in fact come to visit, and on the reasonable assumption that they wanted to be "good parents." This plan was devised with these behavioral and attitudinal constants in mind. Given his recent calamities, Job knew he could *not* count on God's willingness to appear to him and God's desire to be "just." These were the great unknowns, yet the success of Job's plan was wholly dependent upon them. Of course, Job was keenly aware of this uncertainty and was dubious about the plan himself. His doubts were reflected in his wish for some unknown arbiter to appear to ensure that the plan had some chance of working. But he had no more reason to expect an arbiter than to expect God's own appearance. No wonder his counselor friends ridiculed his plan as based on wishful thinking. And they were right. The plan, with its litigation scenario, never materialized. It may have provided some emotional catharsis, but it was completely ineffective as far as Job's difficulties were concerned.

GOD REFRAMES THE SITUATION

God's reframing can be viewed in light of the attempted solutions which preceded it. Against these earlier attempts, everything that God did was paradoxical. God did not address Job's suffering or his alleged guilt, much less enumerate his iniquities. Nor did God respond to Job's allegations. *Why* questions were totally avoided. The reasons for Job's difficulties were not addressed and their causes were not disclosed, probed, or analyzed. *Why* these things happened to Job remain as much an unknown after God's intervention as before. The *what* takes absolute precedence over the *why.* As Rudolf Otto points out, "The Book of Job ... is not so much concerned with the *awefulness* of the majesty [of God] as with its *mysteriousness;* it is concerned with the nonrational in the sense of the irrational, with sheer paradox baffling comprehension, with that which challenges the 'reasonable' and what might be reasonably expected, which goes directly against the grain of reason."[9]

In effect, God refused to enter into any discussion about Job's sufferings and the reasons for them. Instead, God took Job on a kind of imaginary world tour.[10] As God proceeded to depict this world, noting several of its oddities and a number of its terrors, Job recovered the sense of life's meaning which he had lost and which no amount of well-intentioned counseling had been able to restore.

Why did this approach work with Job? According to Watzlawick, Weakland, and Fisch's theory of change, it worked because it did not follow the approach of previously attempted solutions (more of the same), but took an opposite approach, violating the common-sense reasoning of these other solutions. Common sense would say that when a person you care about is suffering, you do not ignore the fact of his suffering but try to do something to help him. Common sense also suggests that you try to discover the reasons he is suffering and use these discoveries in your efforts to help. But God went against this commonsensical approach. God did not focus on Job's difficulties at all, nor did God address the issue of Job's guilt, one plausible explanation for his difficulties. On the contrary, God talked about almost everything else in the world (including the weather!). Job's difficulties—his inexplicable sufferings—were so totally ignored that we can only conclude this was a deliberate action on God's part.

Yet, God's very refusal to talk to Job about his difficulties reframed the situation as viewed by the counselors and by Job himself. As the previous attempts to solve the problem made clear, nothing was to be gained from discussing Job's sufferings and the reasons for them. Job was ready for a different approach, and God obliged. If self-examination had not worked, maybe a distraction would. So, God conceived the idea of taking Job on an imaginary world tour. As they proceeded on this make-believe journey, God made a point of noting the difficulties and challenges of governing a world. Since both Job and God were governors, God was focusing here on a subject that was significant for them both and central to their own vocational identities. By talking to Job of these matters, God affirmed their co-creator relationship, and in this way re-awakened Job's sense of vocation for the world. Thus, God reframed the situation by ignoring whatever rift there had been between them, and instead focused on what the two of them shared together—their concern for the fate of the world. In this way, God redirected Job's thinking away from himself and his own needs, to the world and its need to be cared for. Job was weaned from his self-absorption and challenged, instead, to renew his generative role in the world, thereby regaining his sense of life's meaning and purpose.[11] In Frankl's terms, Job's new identity as co-creator with God provided a new basis for creative value, which led, in turn, to new possibilities for experiential value. The result, attitudinally, was that Job had become a new man. His sense of righteousness, which had been so central to his self-understanding, was no longer based on his personal achievements alone but on his participation with God in the creative maintenance of the world.

One reason this approach worked is that God avoided the issue that had placed Job in a double-bind. If God had focused on the issue of Job's suffering and had proposed still another way for him to commit his case to God, this action would only have increased Job's sense of powerlessness, of being caught in a hopeless paradox of having to call upon his enemy for aid. But God did not expect Job to beg for mercy. In God's view, Job was not obligated to seek help from the very one he suspected of being the cause of his difficulties. God would not expect him to act in a hypocritical, cynical manner. Nor would God require Job to make a confession of guilt which he could not mean, or a confession of faith which he did not believe.

On the other hand, God did want Job to recover his sense of life's meaning and purpose, and helped him to regain this by taking him on an imaginary journey, intimating as they went, that Job could be an important ally in God's efforts to govern the world. God did not say that the world would go to hell if God were not assisted by mortals like Job, but God did invite Job to assist in the task of enabling the world to become what it was intended to be. Thus, God's response was invitational, and Job responded by putting aside talk of litigation against God and "dust and ashes" talk about himself, returning instead to productive labor in the world's behalf. By formulating and enacting this alternative plan, God followed no identifiable precedent or existing formula. God developed it for this occasion, and this occasion only. In so doing, God demonstrated creative gifts, and provided all the evidence that Job required to acclaim God as the ultimate source of all creative acts (42:2).

CONCLUSION

In chapter 6, we saw that the counseling methods employed by Job's counselors were theologically deficient. Is there a theological strength, implicit in the reframing method, that accounts for its effectiveness with Job? I certainly believe so. Of course, the reframing method is not overtly theological, but a particular view of God is especially congenial to it. This is the view that God is a paradox. To the author of the book of Job, God is not a wholly rational God, but neither is God wholly irrational. God is a God of *paradoxical intentions.* To Job, before his encounter with God, God was inconsistent: one moment a friend, the next moment an enemy. But to say that God is inconsistent is to miss the deeper truth that God is, instead, a paradox. As Rudolf Otto points out, such paradox is the heart of the mystery, the strange "beyondness" of God.[12]

In *Answer to Job,* Jung implied the paradoxical nature of God when he noted the "antinomies" within God's nature, and contended that the book of Job presents God as a duality: as blind power on the one hand and enlightened wisdom on the other.[13] To Jung, God as blind power dominates the story of Job, for God terrifies Job into abject submission. Our analysis of the "dust and ashes" passage and emphasis on Job's relation to God as co-creator shows that Jung is wrong, that God as enlightened wisdom pre-dominates. But Jung's basic insight that antinomies exist in God is clearly on target, as it supports the view that God is a God of paradoxical intentions.

Reframing is based on the self-conscious use of paradox. God's intervention worked with Job where the counselors' did not, because God was fully aware that God's own approach to Job was paradoxical. Such awareness of intention means that God's therapeutic intervention was not an exercise of manipulative power or intimidation but of wisdom—the wisdom of self-knowledge (i.e., "I am paradoxical by nature"). The result was Job's recovery of his sense of life's meaning and purpose: a constructive attitude reflected in his shedding of dust and ashes; a sense of doing worthwhile things in his new status as co-creator with God; and satisfying experiences as he lived another hundred and forty years and died "an old man, and full of days" (42:17). Because the book of Job portrays God as directly intervening with Job, eschewing an intermediary, it offers an unusually clear picture of the theology that underlies the reframing method.

This theology makes the daring affirmation that God acts toward the world with paradoxical intentions. Job, who was eventually able to see the two sides of God the Seeing Eye and God the Hunter, was able to appreciate—indeed, was forced to acknowledge—the paradoxical nature of God. Aware of the great gulf that separated him, a mortal self, from God, the eternal self, he was able, nonetheless, to see that they shared their paradoxicality in common. Apparently, his three counselor friends never saw God as Job saw God, perhaps because they never saw themselves as Job saw himself (i.e., as deeply paradoxical—a righteous man by any rational standard, but one who, in his darker, irrational moments, experienced a profound sense of personal shame and self-loathing). And so his friends were condemned to working, perhaps for the rest of *their* days, for first-order change. Awareness of God, and awareness of ourselves, as paradox, is the theological core of pastoral counseling as it reframes for second-order change.

CHAPTER EIGHT
The Wise Fool Reframes

Alastair V. Campbell identified three images of the pastoral care giver: the shepherd, the wounded healer, and the wise fool.[1] The shepherd is associated with the views of Seward Hiltner, who emphasized the shepherding perspective in *The Christian Shepherd* and *Preface to Pastoral Theology*.[2] The wounded healer is the image proposed by Henri Nouwen in his book entitled *The Wounded Healer*.[3] The wise fool image is based on Heije Faber's comparison of the minister in the hospital to the clown in the circus.[4] Campbell expands on Faber's insightful metaphor in his discussion of the ministry of wise folly.

As one reads this discussion, one sees that the art of reframing is most congenial to the wise fool approach to pastoral care. As shepherds guide and wounded healers empathize, wise fools reframe. Reframing is the very lifeblood of wise-fool ministry.

In earlier writings on Campbell's three types, I have said that the wise fool image undergirds the revisionist model of pastoral care.[5] For this model, problems are addressed by looking at them in a new way, from new, unaccustomed perspectives. The reason we are unable to deal with a problem is that our angle of vision is wrong, narrow, or distorted. By seeing the problem in a radically different way, we discern, through this very seeing, how it may be resolved or that it is not a problem after all.

I said further that one way to gain such a perspective is to imagine how God views the problem, and so consider it from God's angle of vision. This perspective is often humbling and chastening because it brings our sins and stupidity to light; but it helps to overcome deception and illusion, and, for the revisionist, the primary goal of the Christian life is to leave deception and follow after truth. I claim that wise fools favor this way of approaching a problem because they challenge our propensity for darkness and deception, and dare us to view our situation from the perspective of God's truth. Wise fools believe that if human problems were viewed more consistently from this perspective, we would see that they are not as complex as they seem. Truth is remarkably simple; error and falsity are unnecessarily complex. The wise fool exemplifies the revisionist model by reversing our customary ways of perceiving the world and ourselves. What we had viewed as folly (uncommonsensical) is now wisdom, and our former wisdom (common sense) is now folly. Such reversals reveal a new world to us, one to which we were previously blind or insensitive.

Like the pastoral images of shepherd and wounded healer, the wise-fool image is profoundly biblical. As Campbell points out, Paul dismisses worldly wisdom as a guide for Christians and elevates the fool instead: "If any among you think they are wise by this world's standards, they should become fools, in order to be really wise" (1 Cor. 3:18). These fools are vulnerable to earthly powers, are often derided and exploited, are treated as scapegoats, and viewed as "the offal of the world, the scum of the earth" (1 Cor. 4:13). Yet, in all societies and all ages, fools have been "the essential counterpoise to human arrogance, pomposity, and despotism." The fool's "unruly behavior questions the limits of order," the fool's "crazy" outspoken talk probes the meaning of "common sense," the fool's unconventional appearance exposes pride and vanity, and the fool's loyalty to "lost causes" undercuts prudence and self-interest.[6] The more we examine such folly, however, the more ambiguous the image of the fool becomes: "Folly is often two-edged, making mockery of good and ill alike, providing malicious and cruel laughter at times, yet also using humor and ridicule to evoke love and concern. Since folly steps outside order, we cannot expect to control it easily—more often it takes us over in a holy or unholy madness."[7]

On the other hand, Campbell wants to "impose some order on the fool's image in order to see its significance for pastoral care." He identifies three aspects or dimensions to the wise-fool image: simplicity, loyalty, and prophecy. I suggest that these three dimensions oppose the mishandlings of difficulties identified by Watzlawick and his colleagues; because they do, the wise-fool image favors the reframing method.

FOLLY AS SIMPLICITY: BEYOND SIMPLIFICATION

How do we know when folly is wisdom and not simply nonsense? One way we know this is that something unexpected or overlooked becomes disclosed. Sometimes the disclosure of the unexpected or overlooked involves seeing complexities that others were unable to see. But the disclosures that we normally associate with wise folly usually result from taking a simpler view of the situation than others have done. This is not the fallacy of *simplification,* which sees no problem when in fact there is one. Instead, this is the ability to recognize that the problem is actually simpler than it has been perceived to be.

Suppose, for example, that a group of co-workers are discussing one of their colleagues, and offering a number of explanations for why Bill is the way he is. One colleague ventures the opinion that Bill "has narcissistic tendencies reflected in his grandiose self-image." Another observes that Bill "has a problem with authority, especially in situations where he is expected to be deferential to persons who hold positions of legitimate authority over him." Another adds that there are "paranoid" features to Bill's personality which cause him to be on guard, especially in situations where the power he holds is unequal to that of the person with whom he is dealing. Then suppose that after these observations have been offered and solemnly affirmed by the group, another of Bill's co-workers, silent to this point, were to blurt out in obvious anger, "The trouble with Bill is that he's a damned liar. I doubt that he's ever told the truth in his life."

This statement breaks the diagnostic frame which had prevailed to this point and places Bill in a wholly different frame of analysis. Where the original frame was "psychological assessment," the new frame is "moral evaluation." The new frame directs attention to something that was overlooked by the psychological assessments of Bill—the simple but important fact that Bill never tells the truth about anything, that nothing he says is credible. This is a simpler view of Bill than the other diagnoses provided, but it is not simplistic. To say that Bill is a "damned liar" is certainly not to minimize the group's frustrations with Bill. On the contrary, it is to challenge the group to look at the problem from an entirely different standpoint and to see another dimension of it. Yet, the force of this particular challenge is that, when viewed psychologically, certain behaviors may look very complex, but when viewed morally, they are simple and straightforward. Could it be that claims to such complexity are little more than rationalizations for duplicitous behavior? The statement, "Bill is a damned liar," in fact challenges the assumption of the psychological assessments that Bill is a very complex person. The statement says, in effect, "I do not believe that Bill is complex. Instead, he is merely duplicitous."

Thus, one characteristic of the "wise fool" is the capacity to see situations as simpler than others have thought them to be. Other pastoral types tend to see situations as complex, involved, or deep-seated. Shepherds focus on the various contextual and systematic factors that may be responsible for the problem, and wounded healers seek to plumb the depths of deep and painful difficulties. Wise fools tend to see problems as much less intricate and complicated. Truth is remarkably simple. Error and falsity are unnecessarily complex.

This does not mean, however, that once the problem's inherent simplicity has been disclosed, it will necessarily be easy to resolve. Often there is an inverse relationship between a simple problem and an easy solution. Suppose that the survival of a couple's marriage depends on the husband's ability to remain faithful to his wife. This is simple: Be faithful and you will save your marriage. But for this particular husband, who has had a series of affairs, this prescription is not easy at all. In fact, being faithful is actually much harder for him than devising intricate game plans and complicated stories designed to deceive his wife about his sexual behavior. The problem itself is quite simple, but the solution is very difficult. It is like the story of Naaman, who was instructed by the prophet to wash in the Jordan River and he would be cured of leprosy. By assuring Naaman that everyone knew he could do difficult things, his servant reframed the situation for Naaman, enabling him to do the simple thing which was otherwise so hard for him.

No doubt, the wise fool will fail to perceive certain facts about situations which shepherds, with their appreciation for complexity, and wounded healers, with their sensitivity to depths, will more readily recognize. It is not that the wise fool is always right and that the shepherd and wounded healer types are always wrong. Rather, we are identifying a characteristic of wise fools, their tendency to view problems as simpler than they appear to others. Unless the wise fool succumbs to simplification (which is the flip side of the danger that shepherds will be guilty of complexification and wounded healers of false profundity), there is usually genuine insight in what the wise fool has to say. Unfortunately, we tend to resent the suggestion that the truth can be remarkably simple. It offends our intelligence to be told that, where our problems are concerned, there may actually be *less* than meets the eye. Thus, the wisdom of the fool is often dismissed because we are offended by it.

Citing examples from history and literature, such as the Sufis of Islam and Prince Myshkin in Dostoevski's novel *The Idiot,* Campbell talks about wise fools' own simplicity, which enables them to expose the insincerity, self-deception, hypocrisy, and corruption of the people around them. Adults who are in full possession of their faculties cannot pretend to possess the simplicity of natural fools like Prince Myshkin; it would be a strange denial of ourselves to want to do so. But the image of folly as simplicity can help us to rediscover the parts of ourselves which have been lost as we learned "adult wisdom," thus opening up more spontaneous ways of relating to ourselves and others.[8] By recovering the child in ourselves, we discover, anew, our capacity to see problems as simpler than others see them. To perceive such simplicity in human problems, however, often requires the capacity to engage in complex analytical reasoning processes. So, the wise fool image is not an excuse for an unthinking, nonreflective approach to ministry. Wise folly calls forth simplicity, not stupidity or simple nonsense.

FOLLY AS LOYALTY: BEYOND UTOPIANISM

In discussing the simplicity of wise folly, Campbell was concerned with the question: "How do we know when folly is a kind of wisdom and when is it simple nonsense?" In approaching folly as loyalty, his concern is not a question but an enigma: the fool's willingness to disregard self out of a higher loyalty. In Shakespeare's *King Lear,* the fool stands by the king's side when everyone else has deserted him, exhibiting "the simple virtue of an unheroic but persistent loyalty."[9] He acknowledges that he may be a fool for staying with Lear when the situation is hopeless, but he is not a knave, one who

> Serves and seeks for gain
> and follows but for form,
> will pack when it begins to rain,
> and leave thee in the storm.
> (Act 2, Scene 4)

There is no shame in being a loyal fool. There is only shame in being a self-serving and faithless knave.

This foolhardy, improvident loyalty is a prominent feature of Jesus' teaching: "Whosoever will give his life for my sake shall find it" (Matt. 16:25). For Campbell, the enigmatic character of such loyalty finds its ultimate expression in the crazy logic of loving those who do you harm: "Love your enemies, do good to those who hate you, bless those who curse you, and pray for those who mistreat you" (Luke 6:27-28). Jesus looks like the "greatest of fools" when he asks God to forgive his accusers and their minions even as they mock him in his suffering. No one, claims Campbell, would allow himself to be exploited this way unless he trusted, beyond all reason, in the ultimate triumph of love. The enigma of the fool's loyalty is that he allows himself to be exploited, as Jesus' enemies exploit him: "There is nothing more easily exploited than the loyalty of a fool."[10]

What enables fools to remain loyal, refusing to "pack when it begins to rain"? Maybe, as Campbell suggests, this is based on trust in the ultimate triumph of love. But I suspect that fools are less utopian than this. Fools do not perceive that they are involved in a situation that, while hopeless now, will somehow be turned around and ultimately lead to triumph. Instead, fools are more likely to stay with a hopeless situation because, as Watzlawick's book title suggests, "the situation is hopeless but not serious." Unlike the utopians who persist in hopeless situations because they believe their cause may ultimately triumph, fools persist because they refuse to take such situations seriously. To put it another way, utopians are in the business of *making* meaning, while fools are more content to let meaning arise where and when it will. As Watzlawick and his colleagues point out, "The search for a meaning in life is central and all-pervasive" for the utopian, "so much so that the seeker may question everything under the sun, *except* his quest itself, that is, the unquestioned assumption that there *is* a meaning and that he has to discover it in order to survive." The authors challenge this overinvestment in the quest for meaning, viewing it as a prescription for a life of unhappiness. They contrast it to the attitude of the King of Hearts in *Alice in Wonderland* who, after reading the nonsensical poem of the White Rabbit, cheerfully concludes: "If there is no meaning in it, that saves a world of trouble, you know, as we needn't try to find any."[11]

Because fools are not overinvested in the quest for meaning but content to let meaning arise where and when it will, they are free to invest in situations which may or may not have an identifiable purpose, logic, or reason. Fools can remain faithful to their King Lears, no matter how crazy the situation becomes, as fools are not distressed because it makes so little sense. The situation is hopeless, but not serious. Utopians believe that the reality they envision is truer than the reality in which they currently find themselves. Fools also envision other realities—many of them—but they are not so sure that these are any truer. They have a healthy mistrust of such envisionings, perhaps because they entertain so many; so they invest instead in the reality which is there for them to see, finding their happiness—and meaning—in it.

A young minister accepted the pastorate of a small urban parish, fully aware that the church was dying and that there was really nothing she could do to save it. However, during her pastorate there, she made the sort of long-range plans that one would make if the future of the church were assured. New programs were initiated, including youth and evangelism programs designed to expand the church's membership. At no time did she seriously entertain the idea that the church could be saved. Yet, for as long as possible, she resisted the efforts of some of the church's leaders to plan for its eventual demise. They asked, "Why start up new programs when you know that our days are numbered?" Any answer she gave them was unpersuasive—meaningless—to them. When the church did close its doors, she knew these leaders had hurt the congregation through their negativism. Yet she also knew that the situation had always been hopeless and that nothing could have been done to turn it around.

This pastor demonstrated the loyalty of the fool. She was not loyal out of some belief in an eventual triumph, present or future. Nor did she anticipate, either at the time or later, that the whole situation would yield some dramatic meaning. The situation was hopeless, and this is all that could be said for it. But she was loyal to it in spite of its hopelessness—and through these very trying times, there were some genuinely happy moments and some meaningful experiences for her and for other members of the congregation. In fact, she can now say that, while she would never want to go through this experience again, it was one of the happiest and truest, albeit saddest, periods in her life.

The fool's loyalty will always be something of an enigma. In hindsight, one might say that the pastor had been exploited—by the official who sent her there and by the leaders who not only undermined her efforts to minister but also tried to make her the scapegoat for the eventual failure. But, not unlike Jesus, the pastor was most exploited by her faith in God, who was the spiritual source of her unwavering loyalty in this hopeless situation. Yet, like Jesus, she did not experience this condition as exploitation. In fact, her unwavering loyalty to God was a sign that she did not consider herself above—or beneath—the playing of God's fool. And she is the happier for it. St. Francis of Assisi, often called God's greatest fool, is universally regarded as the happiest of God's saints.[12]

If folly as "simplicity" supports reframing by discerning that problems are simpler than they appear, folly as "loyalty" supports reframing by rejecting common sense reasons for avoiding hopeless situations. Common sense says, "Stay away from hopeless situations because you will be dragged down by them." Folly as "loyalty" challenges such common sense and perceives the situation for what it is: a hopeless situation, but not necessarily an unhappy one. King Lear's fool reframes by exhibiting loyalty which has no justification. The failure to extricate oneself from a hopeless situation is a common description of a fool; but through their loyalty, fools offer a different perspective on such involvement. For them, the issue is not whether we know a hopeless situation when we see it, but whether we know the difference between loyalty and knavery. The fool, for no other reason than simple loyalty, will not "pack when it begins to rain, and leave thee in the storm."

FOLLY AS PROPHECY: ESPOUSING PARADOX

If the first two dimensions of folly—simplicity and loyalty—portray the fool as a person of pathos, the third—prophecy—presents a more active, resilient, challenging, and even aggressive fool. As Campbell points out, "The prophetic aspect of folly has, throughout the ages, functioned as a form of challenge to the accepted norms, conventions, and authorities within a society."[13] Prophecy comes across as folly because it "does not fit in with the 'common-sense' assumptions of the day: it cuts cross-grained to earthly power and authority, announcing God's judgment upon it. Thus it is often misunderstood, ridiculed, or simply ignored."[14]

Various Hebrew prophets were viewed as crazy fools: Isaiah, who went naked for three years to warn of the impending humiliation and captivity of Egypt and Cush; Hosea, who married a prostitute and gave ominous names to his children; and Jeremiah, who walked around with a yoke on his back. It is no wonder that Hosea was accused of being a crazy fool, or that Jeremiah was in danger of being locked up as a madman.[15] And Jesus' prophetic acts—e.g., throwing the money lenders out of the temple—evoked the public judgment that he, too, was a crazy fool.

Folly is a potent form of prophecy because it allows us to see ourselves in a clearer light and prevents us from giving fallible human institutions the honor they are *not* due. On the other hand, Campbell warns against assuming that all folly is prophetic: "Clowning, buffoonery, and satire can often be heartless, destructive of human values, a weapon to protect the perpetrator against any genuine involvement with others."[16]

Prophetic folly works through paradox. It involves inverting and thereby subverting the common-sense assumptions of the day. Thus, Jesus uses paradox as he reverses the accepted religious values, making the humble tax-gatherer more righteous than the law-abiding Pharisee, and the Samaritan more compassionate than the priest and Levite. For Campbell, the major vehicle for Jesus' prophetic role as teacher is his use of paradox. What makes him a wise fool, and not just anybody's fool, is that he uses it self-consciously, by design and not by accident.

The image of the wise fool is itself paradoxical—*wise* and *fool* are juxtaposed to one another. The wounded-healer model, which juxtaposes *wounded* and *healer,* is also paradoxical, especially as it draws attention to the power of weakness and vulnerability. But Campbell sees more of paradox in the wise fool.[17] For the wise fool, there is paradox in every facet of human existence, not only in the power of weakness, but also in the success that derives from failure, the dangers that come from playing it safe, the questions that are implied in answers, the answers implied in questions, the sorrows of joy, the joys of sorrow, and so forth. For the wise fool, the parable of the ostrich is a hymn to life itself. In her glory and her stupidity, the ostrich symbolizes existence as the wise fool knows and perceives it. It is not that our lives are hopelessly complex, or wondrously profound, but that they are paradoxical to the core. Among Jesus' own parables, the one that best expresses this view of life is the story of the rich fool. Just when he has achieved a life of economic security, he is told his life is in immediate jeopardy, that he will not survive the night (Luke 12:16-20). This is paradox, and it is no academic matter. It is real. It is life itself. But the rich fool did not see the paradox, where the wise fool—the story teller—did, possibly because he knew that he faced a similar fate, that when least expected, his life, too, would be required of him. A wise fool is one who sees the paradox of her own life as clearly as she sees it in the lives of others.

What makes prophecy paradoxical? The deepest paradox in the prophetic is simply this: The prophet who claims to speak for God cannot know what he is talking about. God's prophet is also God's fool, because God's prophet cannot speak with any certainty. Take Jonah, for example. Jonah, a prophet, knew that God could make a fool of him; by causing Jonah to eat his words, God did. Jonah prophesied that "yet forty days, and Nineveh shall be overthrown!" (3:4). Forty days came and went, but Nineveh remained as secure as ever. Wise to God, Jonah could see that he had played God's fool: "I pray thee, Lord, is not this what I said when I was yet in my country? That is why I made haste to flee to Tarshish; for I knew that thou art a gracious God and merciful, slow to anger, and abounding in steadfast love, and repentest of evil" (4:2). Unlike the self-fulfilling prophet, who avoids playing God's fool by refusing to make falsifiable predictions, Jonah had played the fool—by saying things on God's behalf that proved utterly wrong and made Jonah look very stupid in the eyes of the public. To speak for God means taking the risk—day after day—that what we say about God, especially about God's intentions for the world, will prove utterly and shamefully mistaken.

Of course, it might be argued that Jonah was wrong only because the Ninevites heard what he had to say and repented of their evil ways. Therefore, he was wrong in fact, but was vindicated because his warnings were heeded and had their desired effect. While this argument may make sense to some of us, it does not satisfy Jonah who was not one bit impressed that his words had an effect on the Ninevites. For one thing, the Ninevites may have been insincere, cynically playing the game of repentance. For another, it was more important to Jonah—for his sense of professional integrity—to be right than to have an effect, especially one as ambiguous as this. If he had aspired only for effect—to be successful—he could have been a prophet whose predictions were so ambiguously stated as to be self-fulfilling. Rather, he wanted very much to be right, to say what is unquestionably true about his God.

But God did not allow him to experience the simple pleasure of having spoken the truth about God. Instead, Jonah was God's fool. He was placed in a position where he had no choice but to speak for God, but had to say things that he actually knew nothing about. Had he taken the opposite approach and assured the Ninevites that God would surely spare them if they repented, he had no assurance that God would do this, either. While God could be a gracious God and merciful, God could also be an exacting God who is no more impressed than Jonah had been by the Ninevites' last-minute and possibly hypocritical conversion. After all, there are times when God is not mocked and will not be played for a fool.

Jonah's dilemma, of course, was that he spoke for a God whose very nature is a paradox: gracious and exacting, merciful and demanding. How does one speak for a paradoxical God? We mean no disrespect for God when we say "with laughter." If God were not a paradox, God's prophets would do well just to be angry. But God is a paradox, and therefore, God's prophets cannot speak, cannot live, without laughter. The story of Jonah has been a source of amusement for countless generations. Its account of the cowardly prophet who flees his prophetic role is the most humorous tale in the Bible, illustrating Campbell's view that prophecy is often carried on the wings of laughter. While we tend to view prophets as speaking in angry and indignant voices, the Jonah story says that prophecy is also filtered through laughter. Of course, for Jonah, the events in Nineveh were no laughing matter. He had played God's fool and was God's angry prophet—so angry, in fact, that he wanted to die (4:3). But, if he could have seen himself as his audience sees him, sulking under a great tree in the middle of the desert, he might have found it within himself to laugh, to see that his own situation, while hopeless, was not as serious as he had taught himself to believe.

If he could have seen the humor of it all, he might have gone from this experience to become a very different kind of prophet: not an angry prophet, but a laughing prophet. Campbell asks: If there is laughter in heaven, isn't it part of our prophetic witness to encourage laughter on earth, and to begin by learning to laugh at ourselves? "Individuals who have a lightness of touch, an informality based on amusement at their own ineptitude, bring the simplest of gifts to others—the releasing power of laughter."[18]

Lightness of touch and the releasing power of laughter are essential to the art of reframing. Otherwise, the art degenerates into a weapon which manipulates and mocks the very ones it means to help, and dehumanizes those who use it. Reframing is not for angry prophets, but for prophets who know the releasing power of laughter. Reframing is for prophets who are wise enough to know that God can get along perfectly well without them, and fool enough to believe that God would never try to go it alone. As the poet, Ranier Maria Rilke, in Job-like bravado, put it:[19]

What will you do, God, when I die?
When I, your pitcher, broken, lie?
When I, your drink, go stale or dry?
I am your garb, the trade you ply,
you lose your meaning, losing me.

Homeless without me, you will be
robbed of your welcome, warm and sweet.
I am your sandals: your tired feet
will wander bare for want of me.

What will you do, God? I am afraid.

So, wise fools embrace simplicity, not simplification, loyalty, not utopianism, and a lighthearted brand of prophecy based on a healthy appreciation and respect for the paradoxical ways of God. Wise fools may not be as indispensable as shepherds, or as deep as wounded healers, but they do not flinch from truth, they do not pack when it begins to rain, and they have an acute sense for the paradoxes of human (and divine) life. Through all this, they see the enormous potential for miracles in ordinary life, and are not too proud to use techniques, like reframings, to see if they may help such miracles happen a bit more often than would otherwise occur by chance. So, perhaps wise fools are to be forgiven for entertaining the thought that God will find this earth a hell of a place to be when they have gone to the place where no one cries— except, shall we say, from uncontrolled laughter?

Notes

Introduction

1. Howard J. Clinebell, Jr., *Basic Types of Pastoral Counseling* (Nashville: Abingdon Press, 1966).

2. Howard J. Clinebell, *Basic Types of Pastoral Care and Counseling: Resources for the Ministry of Healing and Growth* (Nashville: Abingdon Press, 1984).

3. Richard Bandler and John Grinder, *Reframing: Neuro-Linguistic Programming* (Moab, Utah: Real People Press, 1979).

4. Paul Watzlawick, John Weakland, and Richard Fisch, *Change: Principles of Problem Formation and Problem Resolution* (New York: W. W. Norton, 1974). For an excellent account of the basic principles of brief therapy, the operation of the center in Palo Alto, and success rates, see John H. Weakland, Richard Fisch, Paul Watzlawick, and Arthur M. Bodin, "Brief Therapy: Focused Problem Resolution," *Family Process* 13 (1974): 141–68.

5. Donald Capps, *Pastoral Care: A Thematic Approach* (Philadelphia: Westminster Press, 1979).

6. I also make use of these works by Paul Watzlawick and his colleagues: Paul Watzlawick, *The Language of Change: Elements of Therapeutic Communication* (New York: Basic Books, 1978); Watzlawick, *The Situation is Hopeless, But Not Serious: The Pursuit of Unhappiness* (New York: W. W. Norton, 1983); Paul Watzlawick, Janet Beavin Barelas, and Don D. Jackson, *Pragmatics of Human Communication: A Study of Interactional Patterns, Pathologies, and Paradoxes* (New York: W. W. Norton, 1967). Other books by Watzlawick include two edited volumes: Paul Watzlawick and John H. Weakland, eds., *The Interactional View* (New York: W. W. Norton, 1977); and Paul Watzlawick, ed., *The Invented Reality* (New York: W. W. Norton, 1984).

7. Donald Capps, *Biblical Approaches to Pastoral Counseling* (Philadelphia: Westminster Press, 1981).

8. Alastair V. Campbell, *Rediscovering Pastoral Care* (Philadelphia: Westminster Press, 1981).

Chapter 1: The Method of Reframing

1. Bandler and Grinder, *Reframing*, 1.

2. Ibid., 1.

3. Sigmund Freud, *Jokes and Their Relation to the Unconscious.* Trans. James Strachey (New York: W. W. Norton, 1963), 49.

4. Bandler and Grinder, *Reframing*, 2.

5. Ibid., 24.

6. Watzlawick, Weakland, and Fisch, *Change.*

7. Ibid., 10–11.

8. Ibid., 31–32.

9. Ibid., 48.

10. Ibid., 50.

11. Ibid., 62.

12. See Watzlawick, Barelas, and Jackson, *Pragmatics,* 200.

13. Ibid., 210.

14. Watzlawick, Weakland, and Fisch, *Change,* 95.

15. Ibid., 81–82.

16. Ibid., 84. The quotation is from Ludwig Wittgenstein.

17. Ibid., 111.

18. Carl R. Rogers wrote an important essay on "perceptual reorganization" that may be regarded as an early formulation of the reframing method. See "Perceptual Reorganization in Client-Centered Therapy," in *Perception: An Approach to Personality,* ed. R. R. Blake and G. V. Ramsey (New York: Ronald Press, 1951), 307–27. I have discussed this article in relation to Jesus' parables and marriage counseling in *Biblical Approaches to Pastoral Counseling,* 182–87.

19. Bandler and Grinder, *Reframing,* 42.

20. Ibid.

21. Ibid.

22. Stephen R. and Carol H. Lankton, *The Answer Within: A Clinical Framework of Ericksonian Hypnotherapy* (New York: Brunner/Mazel, 1983), 336–37.

Chapter 2: The Techniques of Reframing

1. Victor Frankl coined the phrase "paradoxical intention." *Man's Search for Meaning: An Introduction to Logotherapy.* Trans. Ilse Lasch (New York: Washington Square Press, 1963).

2. Elisabeth Lukas, *Meaningful Living: Logotherapeutic Guide to Health* (New York: Grove Press, 1984), 79–81.

3. Ibid., 82–83.

4. Watzlawick, Weakland, and Fisch, *Change,* 80–81.

5. Viktor Frankl originated the technique of dereflection. See *Man's Search for Meaning.*

6. Watzlawick, Weakland, and Fisch, *Change,* 100–101.

7. Ibid., 124–27.

8. Ibid., 130–33.

9. Ibid., 133–40.

10. James E. Dittes, *The Church in the Way* (New York: Scribners, 1967), Dittes, *When the People Say No* (San Francisco: Harper and Row, 1979).

11. Watzlawick, Weakland, and Fisch, *Change,* 142–46.

12. Ibid., 108–17.

13. Jay Haley, *Uncommon Therapy* (New York: W. W. Norton, 1973), 25–26, 298–99.

14. Clinebell, *Basic Types of Pastoral Counseling,* 109–13.

15. Watzlawick, *The Language of Change,* 150–52.

16. Recounted in Harvey Mindess, *Makers of Psychology: The Personal Factor* (New York: Human Sciences Press, 1988), 141–42.

17. Therapists who reframe sometimes use what Stephen Lankton calls an "ambiguous function assignment," which involves giving the client an assignment to do (involving an action with one or more objects) and then asking the client the following week, "Why do you think I asked you to do this?" The therapist does not have a reason for this particular assignment but is using it to encourage the client to do some creative thinking of her own about her problem. A pastor may use the Bible in this way, having counselees read a suggested biblical passage (particularly a story) that is not related to the counselees' problems in any obvious way, but that stimulates them to think creatively about their problems as they attempt to guess why the pastor assigned this particular passage. See Stephen R. and Carol H. Lankton, *Enchantment and Intervention in Family Therapy* (New York: Brunner/Mazel, 1986), 136–52.

18. Jay Haley, *The Power Tactics of Jesus,* 2nd. ed. (Rockville, Md.: The Triangle Press, 1986), 39–43.

19. A less extreme technique is storytelling. As Bill O'Hanlon and James Wilk point out in *Shifting Contexts: The Generation of Effective Psychotherapy* (New York: The Guilford Press, 1987), "If a therapist finds that a client is taking over the negotiations, the therapist can gently, politely, but powerfully regain the floor by telling a story. As the story is unknown to the client, the client cannot take over its telling, and since it is not clear what the point of the story is going to be, the client cannot begin to 'contest' it" (p. 173).

20. Stephen R. and Carol H. Lankton, *The Answer Within,* 338.

Chapter 3: Reframing: The Ministry of Jesus
1. Watzlawick, *The Language of Change,* 119.
2. Ibid., 124.
3. Case cited in Watzlawick, ibid., 133–35.
4. Ibid., 125.
5. Bandler and Grinder, *Reframing,* 42.

Chapter 4: Superficial Counsel—A Case Study
1. Jay E. Adams, *The Use of the Scriptures in Counseling* (Grand Rapids: Baker Book House, 1975), 81–83.
2. Bandler and Grinder, *Reframing,* 42.

Chapter 5: Healing Utopia—A Case Study
1. Watzlawick, Weakland, and Fisch, *Change,* 152.
2. Ibid.
3. Ibid., 153–54.
4. John Dominic Crossan, *In Parables: The Challenge of the Historical Jesus* (New York: Harper and Row, 1973), 37–52.
5. R. Waelder's concept of the "average expectable environment" is discussed by Heinz Hartmann in *Ego Psychology and the Problem of Adaptation* (New York: International Universities Press, 1958), 55; and by Robert W. White in *Ego and Reality in Psycho-analytic Theory* (New York: International Universities Press, 1963), 16.
6. Watzlawick, *The Situation Is Hopeless But Not Serious,* 23.
7. Evidence that reframing methods are appropriate for use by parish pastors is the Doctor of Ministry thesis by Douglas J. Green, "Solving Parish Problems: Applying the Mental Research Institute's Brief Therapy to Counseling, Administrative, and Preaching Problems" (Ithaca, N.Y.: Colgate Rochester Divinity School, 1989). In addition to pastoral care and counseling cases, Green provides some extremely interesting examples of the use of reframing techniques in the solving of organizational and administrative problems. He also addresses objections to reframing methods for ethical reasons, noting that most such objections tend to be hypocritical or based on an unrealistic view of pastor-laity relationships. (See especially chapter 4.)

Chapter 6: The Inadequate Methods of Job's Counselors
1. Clinebell, *Basic Types of Pastoral Care and Counseling,* 170–71.
2. Ibid., 171–72.

3. Ibid., 174.

4. See Norman C. Habel, *The Book of Job: A Commentary* (Philadelphia: Westminster Press, 1985), 135.

5. Clinebell, *Basic Types of Pastoral Care and Counseling,* 173–74.

6. Ibid., 171.

7. Judith A. Cook and Dale W. Wimberley, "If I Should Die Before I Wake: Religious Commitment and Adjustment to the Death of a Child," *Journal for the Scientific Study of Religion* 22 (1983): 222–38.

8. Gordon W. Allport, *The Individual and His Religion* (New York: Macmillan Company, 1950), 58–59.

9. William James, *The Varieties of Religious Experience* (New York: Mentor Books, 1958), chs. 4–5.

10. Clinebell, *Basic Types of Pastoral Care and Counseling,* 177.

11. Ibid., 184.

12. Howard W. Stone, *Crisis Counseling* (Philadelphia: Fortress Press, 1976), 32–48.

13. See Clinebell, *Basic Types of Pastoral Care and Counseling,* 205–208.

14. David K. Switzer, *The Minister as Crisis Counselor,* rev. ed. (Nashville: Abingdon Press, 1986), 65–89.

15. Clinebell, *Basic Types of Pastoral Care and Counseling,* 199.

16. Ibid., 188.

17. Ibid., 190

18. David K. Switzer, "Crisis Intervention and Problem Solving," in *Clinical Handbook of Pastoral Counseling,* ed. Robert J. Wicks, Richard D. Parsons, and Donald Capps (New York: Paulist Press, 1985), 135.

19. Habel, *The Book of Job: A Commentary,* 177.

20. Ibid., 194.

21. See Erving Goffman, *Stigma: Notes on the Management of Spoiled Identity* (Englewood Cliffs, N.J.: Prentice-Hall, 1963).

22. Switzer, "Crisis Intervention and Problem Solving," 135.

23. For efforts to explore the theological implications of shame within a pastoral care context, see Donald Capps, *Life Cycle Theory and Pastoral Care* (Philadelphia: Fortress Press, 1983), ch. 4. Also John Patton, *Is Human Forgiveness Possible?* (Nashville: Abingdon Press, 1985).

24. Clinebell, *Basic Types of Pastoral Care and Counseling,* 139.

25. Ibid., ch. 14.

26. Ibid., 140.

27. Ibid., 141.

28. Ibid., 142.

29. Ibid., 153.

30. Ibid., 154.

31. Ibid., 159.

32. Quoted in Clinebell, ibid.

33. Ibid.

34. Ibid., 255.

35. Ibid., 256.

36. Quoted in Clinebell, ibid., 257.

37. Habel, *The Book of Job: A Commentary,* 318.

38. Watzlawick, *The Language of Change,* 120–21. Also see Viktor Frankl, "Paradoxical Interventions," *American Journal of Psychotherapy* 14 (1960): 520–35.

39. Harold S. Kushner, *When Bad Things Happen to Good People* (New York: Avon Books, 1981).

Chapter 7: God Reframes for Second-Order Change

1. Habel, *The Book of Job: A Commentary,* 517.

2. Ibid., 529.

3. Ibid., 532.

4. Ibid., 547.

5. David Bakan makes precisely this point in his consideration of the parable of the ostrich, *Disease, Pain, and Sacrifice* (Chicago: The University of Chicago Press, 1968), 107–108.

6. Habel, *The Book of Job: A Commentary,* 564.

7. Ibid., 583.

8. The theme of Job as "co-creator" with God is emphasized by J. Gerald Janzen, *Job* (Atlanta: John Knox Press, 1985), 257–59.

9. Rudolf Otto, *The Idea of the Holy.* Trans. John W. Harvey (London: Oxford University Press, 1958), p. 100.

10. God's taking of Job on an imaginary world tour may be viewed as an example of the therapeutic use of "enchantment." Cf. Stephen R. and Carol H. Lankton, *Enchantment and Intervention in Family Therapy.*

11. Erik H. Erikson, *Childhood and Society,* 2nd. rev. ed. (New York: W. W. Norton, 1963), 266–68.

12. Otto, *The Idea of the Holy,* p. 173.

13. C. G. Jung, *Answer to Job.* Trans. R. F. C. Hull (Princeton: Princeton University Press, 1973).

Chapter 8: The Wise Fool Reframes

1. Campbell, *Rediscovering Pastoral Care.*

2. Seward Hiltner, *The Christian Shepherd* (Nashville: Abingdon Press, 1959); Hiltner, *Preface to Pastoral Theology* (Nashville: Abingdon Press, 1958).

3. Henri Nouwen, *The Wounded Healer* (Garden City, N.Y.: Doubleday and Company, 1972).

4. Heije Faber, *Pastoral Care in the Modern Hospital* (Philadelphia: Fortress Press, 1984), 70–81.

5. Donald Capps, *Pastoral Care and Hermeneutics* (Philadelphia: Fortress Press, 1984), 70–81. The revisionist model is one of three pastoral care models presented in this book. The others are the contextualist, which is associated with the shepherd image, and the experientialist, which is related to the wounded healer image.

6. Campbell, *Rediscovering Pastoral Care*, 55.

7. Ibid., 55–56.

8. Ibid., 58–59.

9. Ibid., 60.

10. Ibid., 62.

11. Watzlawick, Weakland, and Fisch, *Change*, 55.

12. Julien Green, *God's Fool: The Life and Times of Francis of Assisi*. Trans. Peter Heinegg (San Francisco: Harper and Row, 1983).

13. Campbell, *Rediscovering Pastoral Care*, 62.

14. Ibid., 64.

15. Ibid., 63–64.

16. Ibid., 65.

17. Ibid., 50.

18. Ibid., 71.

19. Ranier Maria Rilke, *Poems from the Book of Hours*. Trans. Babette Deutsch (New York: New Directions Publishing Corporation, 1941), p. 31.

Index of Scripture

Index of Subjects and Authors